Comprehensive Capricorn ©
A Complete Guide

By
Best Selling Author
Dr. Manifest

DEDICATION

The writing of this book was inspired, not only by my love of those born under the zodiac sign of Capricorn, but my love of humanity; in wanting to make a positive contribution to the world, that could in some way help, enlighten, educate and inspire others. I dedicate this book to all those who encouraged and supported not only my writing gift and ability, but my advancement as a man and a human being. First and foremost I dedicate this book to THE MOST HIGH GOD with whom nothing is possible and who led me in the spirit to finally write this book by His grace, and present it to the world. My mother, Evangelist Kathleen R. Fludd who loved, supported and encouraged me from day one and never wavered; My two best male friends in the whole world, who are more like my brothers because they never turned on me nor was ever jealous of me and my abilities, Tony F. and Joshua (Bucky, my longest tenured friend and still active in my life); Martine, who was always more than a manager to me and someone I will always have a profound love and respect for, Tina, my 2nd longest tenured friend, still active in my life, we go way back to when we were 12 and 13 years old, love you much and appreciate your continued love and support. Silky Slim, who believed in my talents, skills and abilities as a top level recording artist, song writer and producer and signed me to my first recording contract! My Uncle Matthew, my brother Tracy and sister Nicky we've been through so much as a family, I love you both. Mona Norvell and Marilyn Arnold (both Capricorns) for inspiring me to keep going and encouraging me to step out with my God given talent for writing after having touched so many around the world through my inspirational words. Last but certainly not least, I dedicate this book to two people who meant more to me than words could ever express, but is no longer with us, My grandfather Eugene Smalls, who taught me what it means to be a man, husband and father and my Aunt, Patricia Ann Williams-Bryant.

Patricia Ann Williams Bryant

TABLE OF CONTENTS

Foreword

First and foremost, For those who may not know me or have ever heard of me, I think it's important to establish from the onset of this book, exactly who I am and what I'm not; That said, I am not an astrologist, star gazer, fortune teller, palm reader, magician, warlock, devil worshipper, necromancer, soothsayer, gypsy, sorcerer, medium or anything along those lines; I'm actually a firm believer in God. No, that is not a contradiction, and I will deal with that a little further down in this foreword. Now that we have that out of the way, let me continue. I'm simply a man who desires to help, inspire, teach and enlighten others. I have been blessed with the spirit of wisdom, but also knowledge as it pertains to the other power of the zodiac, that is almost never talked about: The behavioral science aspect of it, and how it can help us become better people, help us make better personal, professional decisions and potentially cut down on divorces, spousal abuse, etc... To a whole lot of people, especially those that identify with the Christian faith, just to say the word astrology or zodiac sparks an immediate negative or defensive reaction, because they've been told and taught that they're not supposed to "believe in it"; and while the notion is partially correct, it is not the complete truth. There is some misinformation there mixed in with some falsehood that I plan to put to rest, hopefully once and for all, and people can stop looking crazy and cross-eyed just because someone asks them what their zodiac sign is. Please understand this however, I am not here to try and convince anyone of anything. There are people who say they don't believe in the power of the zodiac, and that' fine. I will use my knowledge to present this book to the world, and it is up to you to read with an open mind and receive the information contained therein or not, that's completely up to you. I dedicate this book to every single Capricorn in the world, regardless of age, gender, ethnicity, social or economic status who seek knowledge, enlightenment and a better understanding of who you are, along with a higher level of consciousness with respect to your very being; what helps makes you who you are, and the age old question; Why do we do the things we do. Additionally, I also dedicate it to those in relationships with a Capricorn, who desire to be in one or has a family or close friend whom you seek to know more about or better understand. I was born under the zodiac sign of Capricorn. For as long as I can remember, I have always been totally fascinated and intrigued with human behavior, philosophy and theology. I entitled this book Comprehensive Capricorn because there has never been a book as detailed as this one with respect to those born under the sign of Capricorn. As with anything that I commit myself to, I've put my heart and soul behind the writing of this book, and although it is my very first offering, I present it to the Universe in sincere hopes that you all not only enjoy reading its contents, but actually consider the work valued. I touch on other things in this book as well like Universal Laws, the power of spoken word, importance of knowing and embracing masculine/feminine roles in relationships, etc... So while this book certainly lives up to its title and is comprehensively Capricorn, I felt a responsibility and duty to use the platform along with my knowledge in other areas, to enlighten and hopefully inspire many of you who are not Capricorns but could still find the information useful or helpful in some way. My writing style is such that, I try not to use a lot of big fancy words, I do however; want my work to still be literary. I have been able to take my natural talent, ability and understanding of human nature, and combine that with years of extensive research and data collection of all 12 signs of the zodiac. There are many factors that help contribute to your behavior, many right in your very own astrological birth chart; that said, as a

Capricorn, you are not going to possess every single trait I touch on in this book, so, with that in mind, what I've done is narrow the traits down that pretty much belong to the majority of Capricorns in existence. I speak on the importance of knowing your moon sign further in the book if you are interested in uncovering the other half of your personality along with the traits you have that are not normally Capricorn. So, with all of that said, to all of you Capricorns, those married to one, dating one, interested in dating one, work with one, family members of one, or friends with one, mount up...I'm about to take you on an incredible journey into the intricate and complex mind of Capricorn.

Comprehensive Capricorn

CAPRICORN IS AN EARTH SIGN
CHAPTER 1

The 12 signs of the zodiac all fall under one of four elements; either fire, air, water or earth. Capricorn (like Taurus and Virgo) is an earth sign. Each element is important because they all align with our different personalities in some way. For example, Sagittarius, Aries and Leo are all fire signs. Fire is associated with "hot temper", fiery, sometimes easy to anger, can be very aggressive, volatile and explosive. Capricorns tend to be more "grounded" and down to earth (no pun intended) Now, Capricorns aren't normally as high strung as say Aries (known as the bullies and fighters of the zodiac), But they are known to have tempers, especially if pushed past what they consider a more than reasonable limit. Earth signs are going to be more family oriented and homebodies for the most part. The thing to understand about how the behavioral science power of the zodiac works is this; when a person is born into the Universe, the exact minute they are born renders them with an exclusive astrological birth chart, with 12 houses of the zodiac attached to their chart. What does this mean? In lay terms there are literally 12 different zodiac signs that contribute In some way to how you behave, how you approach things emotionally (or lack thereof), etc...In astrology, your moon sign represents your emotional side and how you approach relationships. Capricorns are generally very distant emotionally and not very expressive, that is unless, like me, they have an emotionally expressive moon sign like Cancer. I go more in depth with respect to why knowing yours and your mate's moon sign is so important, especially as it relates to compatibility. Here's a basic breakdown of all 4 elements and what they mean for each sign collectively:

Earth Signs- Earth signs are going to be more practical in nature, methodical, family oriented and homebodies, that are more comfortable in close, familiar or intimate surroundings. Very grounded, down to earth, dependable and level headed. Most of your earth signs make excellent leaders because of their ability to orchestrate and put things together. Virgos tend to act motherly with everyone by telling them what they need to do and offering unsolicited advice. This tends to rub a lot of people the wrong way with them because it gives off a "know it all" appearance at times; many of them mean well, that's just how they're astrologically built and can't help it; Virgos can also be really self-absorbed, nitpicky and fault-finding. However, Virgos are very dependable, level headed and tend to have a great moral compass; if you date a Virgo female you better have your hygiene and health in order. Smokers don't even think about it. Capricorns, the goat, are normally blessed with wisdom and tend to base things on logic and reason. They're very no nonsense and will let you know under no certain terms, they have no time for games or foolishness. Don't take their cool, calm demeanor as some sort of invitation to come at them wrong, because you will find out instantly that you made a huge mistake. Capricorns can be extremely intolerant, and without an emotionally expressive moon sign, tend to be emotionally distant and somewhat detached. Capricorns are very generous, hardworking, family and goal oriented, extremely loyal and whoever invented the term "ride or die" must have had them in mind. They are the rock and leader of the zodiac, who starts and ends each year for good reason. Taurus, while down to earth and practical can be very stubborn but are not to be messed with or messed over either. They tend to love the finer things in life, and Taurus women like Pisces can really be into their appearance, hair and nails done, dressed down, house looking right and they're very loyal once committed. Aside from their stubborn nature, Taurus are very protective of their families, and they are not the ones you really want to lock horns with; Just like their earth brother Capricorn, don't let the smooth taste fool you, they will not be bullied or taken advantage of by anyone, and have no problem standing up for themselves.

Fire Signs- are literally the hell raisers of the zodiac. Aries are infamous for being impatient, love to push people's buttons and are considered the fighters of the zodiac, They don't know how to leave things alone and will push and push until there is some type of explosion, hence them being the "fighters of the zodiac". Aries are normally very fiery, volatile, and dare I say courageous. An Aries will not back down from anyone and they welcome a "good fight", they're just not built like that, but what rubs people the wrong way, most about Aries is their extremely volatile and high strung natures. Nobody likes a bully, and Aries come off as bullies to people. They're very outspoken, and sometimes don't use good discretion; they're also very hard headed and tend to go about doing things their way with no help from you, no matter how much more it makes sense. Just like with Sagittarius, with Aries you either hate them or you love them, there's no middle ground. They love to explore new things and have fun, and don't have much use for rules or regiments. They tend to get bored easily, so you laid back, sensitive, stay at home types need not apply, you will not hold their attention for long. Men, if you're not careful, some Aries women will try to reverse the roles and treat/talk to you like you're the woman if you allow this. You have to be very assertive with Aries cause if you let them run over you? They will, and oh by the way, will not respect you for letting them do that. Sagittarius has a mouth problem, because they have no filter, meaning, if they think it? They'll say it, no worry or concern for how it comes out, rather it will offend, disrespect, belittle or not, That's just how they are; whoever invented the term "brutal honesty" definitely had a Sagittarius in mind. It's difficult for a Sagittarius to maintain a long, meaningful relationship with anyone because they want to do what they want to do. There's no middle ground with Sagittarius, either you hate them or you love them. They tend to make a lot of enemies, crazy thing about that though, is they really don't even care. They love to travel and learn new things. Make excellent conversationalists, but you weaker, sensitive souls beware; Sagittarius tend to say whatever is on their mind and don't believe in filters (for their mouth that is). That said, if you're extra sensitive, you may want to reconsider getting involved with a Sag, cause it's pretty much a guarantee, they will offend you or hurt your feelings, it's a given with them and you can bank it; Sometimes intentionally and sometimes on accident, just being themselves. Leos (males) are arrogant, (females) bossy stay on the go. Their symbol is the Lion for good reason, they love to be on the hunt, and conquering as many women as they can, is what drives Leo male. Leo men normally make great dads, but as husbands they have issues in that department because of that little infidelity thing, They tend to really love and hold their moms in high regard. Leo women aren't normally as promiscuous as the males, they got this kind of attitude about them, the way they carry themselves like they're all that and a bag of chips. I am not mad at them though, they are fiercely loyal once they commit and they're not into any games at all, Leo women are about that life for real, oh yeah they love to be in control too, maybe that's why a lot of them like being on top during sex. The fire signs don't deal well with emotion, and to deal with sensitive, emotional people are not their thing. The fire signs are arguably the most adventurous of all the signs and are extremely social. It's rare to find a Leo who actually likes to stay in the house.

Water Signs- Well when you think water, it equates to tears or emotions, so it's not a stretch that water signs are going to be the more emotional ones of the zodiac. Now Scorpio, while they can be emotional, are really, better known for their quick, hair trigger temper and could very easily have been a Fire sign because of this; but they are extremely loyal, yet prone to revenge when they feel really hurt or betrayed by someone, and Scorpios can be very scathing and hurtful with their tongue. The biggest knock against Scorpios are that they tend to be very possessive, and that can turn into jealousy, real easily. The whole myth and aura about their sexual side is pretty much true, but you finding out about it is something else altogether; meaning, they don't normally just jump right into bed with any and everybody. Cancers are the sweethearts and tend to cling (crab/claws- get it?) once they've gotten attached to someone. They are also called the "cry-babies" of the zodiac because they tend to be really emotional and approach just about all things in their life from that perspective. A lot of signs can't deal with this, especially the Air signs who tend to look at things objectively, and the fire signs who does not have time to hear Cancer crying about something all the time. Cancers are very loyal, committed and love to nurture their loved ones. Pisces are the peace makers of the zodiac, and I never understood this trait, but the absolute biggest knock against Pisces is their tendency to stretch the truth, I mean they lie about things they don't even have to lie about, but that aside, they actually make great and loyal fiends, once you get past their secretive nature. Very non-threatening and spiritually embraceable; and while they can be very emotional, the other thing people don't like about Pisces is they are not very easy to get to know and appear as though they're hiding something, even if they're not. When you first meet a Pisces female, she'll tell you as little as possible, almost like pulling teeth trying to get stuff out of them at first. If they feel pressured, they'll simply disappear, I mean fall off the face of the earth leaving you wondering what the hell just happened.

Air Signs- As intelligent and as objective as many of them are, they're actually prone to having a lot of blond moments. Air-sign/Air head, see the correlation? Of the Air signs, Geminis and Aquarius both love to be stimulated intellectually, but Gemini is the more talkative of the two. Now, just like Libra and Aquarius, Geminis are not emotional and very aloof and standoffish to emotional things. If you're a super sensitive or emotionally needy type, an Air sign is definitely not for you, trust me. Next to Capricorn, nobody is about their money more than an Aquarius, They might have invented the phrase "get money"... even if they are notoriously cheap. Women Aquarius tends to be cheaper than Aquarian men. They look for the bargain in everything, which can get to be really annoying. Libras tend to be extremely talented and have a gift, love or penchant for music (Eminem, Jermaine Dupri, Toni Braxton, Russell Simmons, Lil Wayne, Young Jeezy. T.I., Keyshia Cole, All Libras) Libras are very non-judgmental, detached emotionally; Libra men tend to be vain and somewhat arrogant. Libra women tend to be very easy to talk to and get along with, they really don't like or do drama, and do desire to get along with everyone. Libras are the scales and definitely need balance in their lives. They are truly the no frills sign, with them, what you see is what you get, and you don't ever have to try and impress them, just be yourself, and you'll be fine with Libra.

CAPRICORNS AS CHILDREN
CHAPTER 2

Capricorns are known as the loners of the zodiac. Without a more socially expressive, outgoing moon sign, or any other sign in our chart that would contribute to us being more outgoing, Caps are normally more introverted by nature. We're homebodies who tend to spend a lot of time at home, where we are most comfortable. If you have several children and one of them happens to be a Capricorn, you will notice, that of all your children, that particular child is more than likely going to be more quiet, observant, exhibit good behavior for the most part (at home and at school) appear very mature for their age and grounded. My mom used to call me a "Little old man" because of my slow, methodical demeanor, my thought process and certain things I would say. A Capricorn child, even if they are not the only child tend to go off, do their own thing and spend a lot of time to themselves. They are normally very creative and their interests involve everything from reading, drawing, music, writing, computers, graphic design, etc. Capricorn children tend to be very mature for their age and very well rounded naturally. I was the middle child of three, and although my brother was older, my mother would give me the responsibilities around the house he should have had. Her thing with that was simple, my older brother didn't display the maturity she felt he should have had, as a result, I was given those "older brother" responsibilities. Needless to say, there were plenty days when we would have to move some furniture behind this appointment by my mom. (Furniture moving is an urban metaphor meaning to scuffle or fight) Since Capricorns aren't known to be bullied or back down from anyone, him and I got into many skirmishes and I gave just as good as I got from him. Capricorn children once fascinated with something tend to become fixated and thoroughly engaged. They tend to love reading and figuring stuff out, on their own. They are normally very independent and "march to the beat of their own drum" at an early age. Some people mistake this quality about Capricorn to be atypical of anti-social behavior, and I guess depending on where you're standing, one could view it that way. However, at the end of the day, they are no more responsible for their physiological or astrological makeup any more than you are. The minute everyone is born into the Universe, We are aligned with the constellations and naturally adopt many of our personality traits from this alignment. Now, human behavior, as I've said before, has always been extremely fascinating to me, while at the same time complex. Reason being, there are several contributing factors that go into help shaping who and what we become, as well as how we turn out. Learned behavior is extremely powerful, and the things we are actually shown and taught as children have a huge impact on us behaviorally, as children, to puberty, and as we make the transition to adults. In this, there is no doubt or debate. Children are extremely impressionable, and why, as parents you need to be extremely careful with what you tell your children, especially on a consistent basis. I have always held personally, that verbal abuse is much stronger than physical abuse, because scars eventually heal from physical wounds, but words once embedded into your psyche tend to stay with and affect you in some way for the rest of your life.

Capricorn children are acutely receptive to verbal and visual stimuli. They take in a lot, but just because they aren't very vocal about it, does not mean they aren't totally aware of exactly what's going on, what's being said, who's doing what, etc. Capricorns are innately driven to stand out and be head and shoulders above anyone else in their chosen field, activity or genre. As children they want to win every game, they want to be the best, vocally or quietly. Coming in second or striving to be anything but the best and top in your field, rather its sports, business, entertainment, hip-hop, etc...is pointless. They tend to be the same exact way as adults and this feeling culminated within them as children.

In astrology, your Moon Sign is the emotional side to your nature. It is determined by your actual time of birth into the world/Universe. This is why no two signs will ever be exactly alike and why two people of the same exact sign can be very different. Everyone pretty much knows what their sun or star sign is (determined by your date of birth) but in not knowing what your Moon Sign is, you are essentially missing the other 50% of your personality; basically you've been going through your entire life knowing only half of yourself, your significant other, etc. Your sun and moon signs go together like air and water, yes, it's that important. Have you ever wondered why some Capricorns are more sensitive than others, as well as displaying other traits that you don't possess or identify with? That's because, the way everyone responds emotionally to things, or react to people and situations, depends a lot on whatever that person's Moon Sign is. To further illustrate my point: My sun sign is obviously Capricorn, right? But my Moon Sign is Cancer. What that essentially means, is that I have some of their personality traits as well, on top of my Capricorn ones. So the fact that I'm a little more sentimental, emotionally expressive, affectionate, etc...all point to being traits of my Cancer Moon, because those aren't traits normally associated with Capricorn, follow me? The same will apply to you once you find out what yours is. Whatever your Moon Sign is? You are going to have some of those traits as well. I have provided the link to a Moon Sign Calculator below so you can find out yours and anyone else who you want to have a much better and more accurate understanding about. Keep in mind though, that calculator acts as any other type of calculator with respect to calculating numbers; If your exact birthday, year and time is correct, so shall the calculation of your Moon Sign be. As long as your numbers are correct and accurate, the results are not open for debate or rather or not you "agree" with it or not. That is exclusively yours, and no other person will have your exact birth chart. If you plug all of your information and your moon sign sounds absolutely nothing like you, I highly suggest you have a little talk with mom or dad about your actual birthday and birth time. Other than that though, Congratulations, you now understand why your traits are so much different than other Capricorns; we all carry the traits of a second sign (Moon sign) and have done so your entire life unbeknownst to you, until now that is. Welcome to the other half of you.

http://www.lunarium.co.uk/moonsign/calculator.jsp

CAPRICORNS AND RELATIONSHIPS
CHAPTER 4

Capricorns hate to fail at anything. I mean it really bothers us internally, to fail. Our relationships are no different. We will do everything in our power to ensure personal relationship success; however, we do have our limits. Once we get to the point of no return, have given it everything we have, and there seems to be no resolution in sight? We're done. I mean, done, done; we're not going to keep rehashing the same thing over and over, the redundancy is annoying plus it's rather pointless, No thanks, and all the best to you with the rest of your life. Clearly, we weren't meant for one another. When looking for a partner, a couple things Capricorns are drawn to are: intelligence, stability, nice-looking, well-kept hygiene, maturity and class. Capricorns aren't normally jealous or possessive, mostly because we don't want to be possessed. We can however, be very territorial, and some get the two confused at times. So, if you're the insecure, jealous type who's emotionally needy, clingy and/or insecure, you will not be a good fit for Capricorn. Capricorns don't expect anything from you that they aren't 100% willing to give or are already giving. If a Capricorn breaks up with you, It's rare there's a rekindling of any romance, because in our mind, Or rather, the way we process things, We gave the relationship everything we had, so to end up breaking up signifies, there is nothing more we can do or give, so to go back to it, is pointless. Inconsistency is one of Capricorn's biggest annoyances. Whatever you are and whatever you do, all we ask is that you be consistent. Capricorns find people who are inconsistent extremely frustrating and nerve wrecking; one minute it's this, the next it's that, take notes all you Air signs, especially Libra and Gemini. Capricorns unfairly get pegged with "being difficult to live with"...Nothing could be further from the truth. All we ask is that you not touch or move our things without our permission and we promise to do the same; Respect our space, we'll respect yours; Don't disrupt our peace when we're having our "quiet time" to ourselves, and basically, we'll be just fine. Yes, we are and can be work-a-holics, but trust me; we don't and won't neglect our responsibilities as someone's "significant other". We are totally aware that there is a level of responsibility attached to being in a committed relationship. Capricorns are not hard to please in a relationship, Plus we give what we expect, fair enough right? All we ask is that you communicate with us openly, honestly and clearly, i.e. we do not like to play the guessing game or kept in the dark about anything, nor can we read your mind, please articulate what's going on from your perspective and let's talk about it. We welcome and respect the truth, no matter how "harsh" it may be. We also expect, what should come automatically with any relationship, loyalty, respect, honor and consideration. While love, at some point is a given, with us, sometimes that takes a while to develop, naturally and organically over time. We thrive on consistency, order and discipline. If you're this way one day, and that way the next, it throws our mental equilibrium off and out of whack, and we simply cannot function this way. If we tell you something, you can take it to the bank; If you tell us something, yet your actions indicate something entirely different, and you do this consistently, What that shows and tells us is that we can't depend on you, we can't trust you and it reeks of instability. This is by no means comprehensive, but it is a nice blueprint for getting into or being in a successful, productive relationship with Capricorn. The nuances of male and female are very similar with slight differences. You don't always have to "understand" how and why your significant other feels a certain way about something. It's not for you to understand all the time, just respect and acknowledge what they feel and don't make them seem trivial or like it's not important. It's not important or trivial to you, but obviously it is to them. If you love and value them, that's one of the worst things you can do in a relationship, make them feel like what they say and think is trivial, unimportant or miniscule. Capricorns, by nature need "private time", doesn't matter what our status is (married, dating, living with significant other, etc.)

We are subject to go into our own little world and don't want to be bothered by anyone for a while. This is just how we "get our mind right" and replenish. Our mates have to really understand this about us and not be offended, or take it personally or eventually this trait would cause problems in our relationships. You can call it "moody" or whatever you like, but this is how we are by nature; you may not understand it, but we simply ask that you respect it. It's rare that a Capricorn cheats in a relationship, but if they do, in their mind they've mentally checked out of that relationship already; which is why if that's the case, go to your mate, sit down, and have that conversation, that way, you're not on the hook to the Universe, and karma won't have to come knocking on your door when you least expect it. You will have to answer and pay for what you did. Capricorns are relationship minded, and prefer to be in one, vice dating a bunch of different people. Truthfully, the whole dating thing is a necessary "evil" almost, we get that, we just don't have that kind of time to devote to the process. Family is extremely important to Capricorn, and why we are so guarded and protective when it comes to ours. Capricorns do tend to have high standards, but we are not hard to please, that's just not true. The exact opposite is actually true for us. If we're into you, all we ask for is respect, honesty, reasonable space and consider our feelings, not just yours. Capricorn, without a really engaging or emotionally expressive Moon Sign is generally reserved and keep what we're feeling inside; So in the beginning stages of dating you might start to wonder if we're even interested; However, it is perfectly possible that we've already "fallen for you" and taking our time to be sure we are ready to commit to a relationship. If a Capricorn commits to something or someone, please believe we take pride in all of our commitments, because if we don't want to commit, we just won't, simple as that. We don't approach anything half-assed; so it's a given, we expect the exact same thing in return if someone commits to us. If you desire to be with a Capricorn Woman, in you, she has to see attractiveness, honesty, stability, intelligence, strength, self-assured but not arrogant, confident, honest, responsible, have a vision and a plan for the future. Capricorn males tend to be the strong, silent types. Considered the "charmers" of the zodiac, we may not say much when we walk into a room but our presence speaks volumes; women say they are attracted to the mysteriousness of the Capricorn male, we're not mysterious though, just very private until we're comfortable enough with you to open up. Contrary to popular opinion, we are not "secretive", we are however very private and will only let you in on things on a "need to know" basis.

CAPRICORNS AND FRIENDSHIPS
CHAPTER 5

It is extremely rare for Capricorn to have a big social circle of friends. The thing is, they may actually know a lot of people, but count very few as actual friends. That's a small, but huge word at the same time for Capricorn. Capricorns are simply not into hanging out and around a bunch of people, especially if they aren't familiar or comfortable with them. As children, they tend to gravitate towards an individual with whom they share the most in common and that's who they'll more than likely form, what would be a lifelong bond and friendship. Trust is not a word taken likely by them, as such, they do not just give someone that unless they have proven themselves to be trustworthy. It is often difficult for Capricorns to forge really close friendships because of the way in which they view those type of relationships. If they consider you a friend, they epitomize what that word means in every sense. Extremely loyal, they would not hesitate to help a friend in need, or even if just to give some great advice to. A lot of Capricorns tend to speak with the spirit of wisdom, and for the most part, they're just real big on common sense. They use reason and logic to solve many of theirs, their friends and loved ones problems. If you actually count a Capricorn as a friend, you have someone who will never leave nor forsake you, even if everyone else in your life does. As long as you don't do anything to betray their trust in a major way, you have an ally for life. Capricorns can be closed off and not seem very approachable or sociable or they can actually be really engaging and the life of the party. Some may see this as a great contrast, but therein lies the complex nature of the goat. To befriend one, it would behoove you to have sincere motives and intentions, even if you don't, nine times out of ten they would be able to discern rather or not your intentions are less than honorable. They tend to be very cautious by nature, so it's rare for them to just jump right into some typed of alliance with you unless you have been tried, true, and are trustworthy (I call it the three t's). We take friendships very seriously and approach them the same as any other serious relationship we've committed ourselves to. For this reason, many Capricorns end up being really disappointed when and if we deem a friend is falling short and not giving us the same type of loyalty in return. This needs to be said as well; If you as a friend, hurt or betray them in a major way, that's pretty much the beginning of the end of your relationship/friendship with them. Some things you may be able to come back from, some you can't. It's not even about holding a grudge, which they're known to do that as well, it's more about having placed your trust and faith in someone, and they betray that in a way there is no rectifying or coming back from. We may forgive you, but that doesn't mean it will ever be like how it was, nor does it mean we will ever physically associate with you again. Once our trust is broken, just like in any romantic relationship, marriage, etc... It's difficult to damn near impossible to regain trust, once lost. I'm not saying it's impossible, but what I am saying, is that for Capricorns if you betray their trust like that, they'll forgive in time and love you from a distance, but make no mistake, they will cut all ties with you; walk right past you like they never even knew you. Once we turn our hearts cold towards someone, it would take an act of God and a new heart to embrace the violator again. We're real big on justice, so if someone does us wrong unjustly or without cause or provocation, we really take it to heart, to the point of even dreaming about it. We despise injustice. It's like it slowly eats away at our very soul. We will give you everything we have, But if you show us that our friendship isn't valued, trust me on this, you will not have 'ole' Capricorn to kick around much longer because we'll be gone out of your life quicker than a New York minute. Capricorns do tend to believe in karma too, what goes around, comes right back around and sometimes tenfold. It may sound cliché', but we believe wholeheartedly in treating others the way you want to be treated. As simple as that sounds, it still boggles my mind how so many people still don't or can't seem to understand that.

CAPRICORN MALES
CHAPTER 6

Capricorn males are normally the strong, silent types. Very grounded, focused, disciplined and not known to make quick or rash decisions at all. Everything is well thought out and planned; and Capricorn male will not move until or unless he feels it's the opportune time to do so. Capricorn males are family oriented and take great pride in being protectors and providers for theirs. Many of them possess great wisdom, which is an excellent trait for leadership, where fair and just decisions have to be made. Normally, they are very composed (even under extreme pressure), efficient and tend to be one of the hardest workers. They are also very cautious by nature; sometimes a little too cautious, to the point of them actually missing out on certain opportunities because of their penchant for wanting to "get it right" study long study wrong right? Oh well, I guess you can't miss what you never had either though right? Right. They thrive on making decisions based on intellect, reason and logic, rarely are they subjective and make decisions based on emotion. That is, unless they possess a more subjective moon sign like Cancer or Pisces. A Capricorn male will set a goal (s) and sometimes slowly, surely and methodically they will make their way up that mountain until they reach the top. Practical and very sensible, they're not into fantasies or "pipe dreams" at all, they're all about preparation, planning and producing tangible results. They tend to be very focused with an "eyes on the prize" mentality that speaks resiliency almost like no other.

Contrary to popular opinion, they are not pessimists; they are realists, who make a conscious decision not to look at the world through rose colored glasses. Sometimes reality is just harsh, and for whatever reason, people generally have a hard time dealing with the harsh reality of a situation; enter Mr. Capricorn, he calls it what it is, and tells you how it is, virtually uncut. He is extremely ambitious, if nothing else; determined, and focused because failure is simply not an option. He'll endure whatever he has to endure because he knows at the end of the rainbow is a big pot of gold. Success is relative to so many things, but so is failure. The benefits of what success brings is not lost on him at all, because with that can come fame, a huge platform with which to be heard, and the obvious, which is money; Which leads me to another gross misconception about Capricorns. Yes, we make no apologies for liking the "finer" things in life and providing material comfort for themselves and their families, however, we are not driven by money. We are driven by the idea of success, and normally with that often come a lot of money. There it is there. Let's not act like having money is a horrible thing either. Wouldn't you rather have it and not need it, than to need it and not have it? Capricorns tend to have this "change the world' mindset and want to make a positive contribution. They have compassionate spirits and are driven to always do what's right even under extreme circumstances. Ladies if you have your eyes fixed on Mr. Capricorn as a potential love interest, there are a couple things you absolutely have to know about them. All Capricorns, both male and female find intelligence extremely attractive and sexy. Capricorns aren't normally impressed by material possessions (cars, homes, money, etc...) but to be a great conversationalist who knows a little bit about multiple things will always be a turn on for them. You also have to have some type of goal (s) and/or ambition. Capricorns normally view those who have no bigger goals or dreams as a turn off. To a man who is ambitious and driven as he is, how can you relate to that and support him in them if you lack those traits and qualities yourself? Physically....Well, let me preface by saying this, there isn't anything "shallow" about having a physical preference. You like what you like, and you don't have to apologize to anyone for that. I encourage everyone to go for what does it for you; it's you that has to wake up and come home to that person potentially for the rest of your life; you'll know her when you see her. Now, with all that said, sexiness, to me comes in all shapes and sizes.

What Capricorn men like physically with women, runs the gamut; for me, being 6'5" and 265 lbs, I tend to prefer thick, voluptuous women, big, curvy bottoms, full lips, and big breasts. Does this mean women who don't necessarily have big butts and whatnot, I won't consider sexy or a turn on? Not at all. I've actually dated smaller women who were very size proportionate and extremely sexy. Sexy isn't just physical, sexy can be ambition, drive, the way a person dresses, walks, talks, carry themselves, confidence, etc...Carrying yourself with dignity, self-respect and class will always be a head turner for Mr. "Cooler than the other side of the pillow" Capricorn (R.I.P. Stuart Scott, One of South Carolina's favorite sons). Very serious and no-nonsense, Capricorn males don't suffer fools gladly and are not to be played with or taken for a joke, on any level. They tend to have a presence that commands attention and respect from everyone regardless of social, political or economic status. For the ladies, this is not to say, they do not have a more laid back, easy going and fun side to their personality; it's just always business has to get handled first, or else we won't be able to relax and unwind. How can we when we have so much stuff to do? It's about knowing your priorities. They have no problem sacrificing short term pleasure for long term success. They are the consummate work-a-holics but they do know how to unwind and have a good time, when it's time for that. Grounded and very responsible minded. Capricorn males don't normally "bust crack head moves" i.e. my little funny hip-hop metaphor that means making irrational and illogical decisions that makes sense to no-one but themselves. Stability is the name of their game. Once committed, he is completely dialed in; because if he didn't want to commit, he wouldn't, simple as that. They take their role as provider and protector seriously. He will ensure all the bills are paid (and on time) and everything operates at home as a well-oiled machine. Most Capricorns are homebodies so you won't have to wonder where he is at 2-3 in the morning. They're about handling their business and don't have time or energy for frivolous BS. If a Capricorn male commits, that's exactly what he will be. Being unfaithful is not normally a thought that permeates the inner workings of their mind.

CAPRICORNS AS PARENTS
CHAPTER 7

Capricorns are very protective and some very guarded when it comes to their children. How they were raised will have some impact on how they raise their children, but for the most part, Capricorns have their own views and ideas on child rearing, which may or may not line up with their upbringing. Being independent minded as children they tend to want to foster that mindset and mentality. They are extremely supportive and very much in tuned with every phase and facet of their development. They tend to be strict, but fair with their children. Order and discipline is the key. They will be held to a higher standard and expected to adhere to those expectations. Some Capricorns are going to be somewhat emotionally detached from their children, but depending on their Moon Sign, others can be very nurturing and emotionally engaging. If not careful however, this can turn into coddling, which isn't necessarily a bad thing, but it can inhibit growth with respect to enabling; preventing the child or children from being more independent minded and less dependent. The challenge many parents will face with children, and not just Capricorns, is that whole "sibling rivalry" thing that's so talked about but rarely, truly understood. I understood retrospectively why my brother was always so selfish and we were as different as night and day. Hard to tell we were actually raised by the same woman. My father was absent in my life, but thankfully my grandfather was extremely instrumental in teaching me much of what I know and practice now as a man. What that means and what constitutes being that and commanding respect, by your actions, not empty rhetoric or a bunch of words that hold no weight. Capricorns as parents will not accept our children being accepting of mediocrity. The goal is to try and strive for greatness; failing is ok, not trying isn't. Apathy is not an excuse for complacency, as that tends to bring about laziness; as such, it is important to Capricorn that they encourage their offspring with all kinds of verbal and educational stimuli, by way of books, movies, etc...so they reach their maximum potential. They want the best for them and work extremely hard to provide for them. However, they want and need them to understand that nothing comes easy and there is responsibility and accountability that goes with the material comfort, perks and quirks we are blessed to provide for them. If you meet a Capricorn, and are interested in pursuing something with him or her, and you know they have a child or children, don't ask them a bunch of questions about them because many of them find that really invasive and it could very well turn them off. You have to sort of let them open up, eventually, about their children, As I said in the intro of this segment, they can be very guarded and protective when it comes to their children. Play it by ear and don't assume anything.

CAPRICORN FEMALES
CHAPTER 8

One of the first things you will notice about a Capricorn female is how she walks with this sort of quiet confidence and assuredness about herself. They're not really into trends, but they have a keen eye for fashion and know what looks good. Ms. Capricorn has a presence about her that makes men take notice and other females too. She, like her male counterparts is very no nonsense and all about her business. If you didn't know her, the first thing you would probably think is that she is either stuck up, full of herself or a little bit of both. I can tell you, you would be wrong on both counts. Nothing could be further from the truth. First off, if they don't know you, yes they have no problem being respectful and cordial, but don't expect them to simply open up to you right away and be this sort of "chatty patty", and you're going to start talking like old friends. Female Capricorns are very careful and selective with whom they befriend or let into their life (especially if they have a child or children). She's the quiet and observant type, although not necessarily unpopular. She likes to win, and quietly views her counterparts as competition whom she totally intends to defeat. She is smart, classy and is usually "up" on a lot of different topics. Capricorn women can be just as ambitious as their male counterparts, but there are also some who are pretty "settled" working a good job, going home, taking care of their family and are pretty comfortable in that routine. Contrary to popular opinion and belief not all

Capricorns are driven by some "higher purpose" and that's perfectly ok too. Capricorn women make excellent wives, as they too prefer to be in committed, monogamous relationships vice dating a lot of different guys; she's just got too much going on for all of that. They are a harmonious blend of toughness, which some could easily mistake as this sort of masculine type energy, but at the same time they possess sexiness and sensuality, that when summoned, can maximize their femininity. Yes, she's tough, no-nonsense, and can be ruthlessly ambitious, but beneath that tough exterior lies a woman who's the true "ride or die" for hers, strong enough to lead, but has no problem letting a man perform those functions provided he has proven himself capable. They know how to take care of their man, as long as their man is taking care of and handling his business you won't have a problem with Ms. Capricorn and she will make you a very happy man. However, If you hesitate or act like a deer caught in the headlights, and derelict in your duties, she will eventually step into the role you were supposed to be filling, then at that point, it's the beginning of the end. Once any woman loses respect for her man, there is definitely going to be a disconnect and the relationship so fragmented, there's no way it can be put back together. Capricorn females are very reserved and have this really cool and unassuming demeanor about 'themselves'; however, when the time is right and they are comfortable with you and/or their surroundings, you will see just how really funny and engaging she can be. You'll be standing there thinking, "Wow, I really had her pegged wrong"! She's not into idle gossip or idle chit chatter, it's pointless and a waste of energy. Another thing about Capricorns (male and female) they're not worried about your business because they're too busy minding their own (and highly suggest you do the exact same thing.)

We are sometimes annoyed easily, which I'm sure could be a complete segment by itself. At the end of the day, we feel time; effort and energy should be productive and actually geared towards something. So, what type of guys does Ms. Capricorn normally go for, or rather, how could you get her attention, alright, first and foremost, your physical appearance must be neat, clean, smell nice, good teeth and just overall presentable. (no run down shoes, no holes in anything, etc...) Capricorns aren't impressed with high priced name brand items; That's great if you have them, great if you don't. To us, many times all that stuff is to cover up a person lacking any real substance. That said, the button down doesn't have to be polo, just as long as it's nice and neat. Capricorn women like a nicely dressed man who has a certain confidence about himself. Approach and speak to her respectfully, don't be vulgar or throw around a bunch of 4 letter words, trust me, that will turn her off instantly! Have some intelligence, or bring up an interesting topic to sort of break the ice. Lady Capricorn loves an enlightened, well versed man who comes off knowledgeable and somewhat multi-cultured. Your education is not so much a big deal or requirement as long as you talk and present yourself like you got some doggone sense. You could have a GED or a PhD, but if you're perceived as not being very bright, it will be a turn off. Don't get too invasive in your line of questioning and keep the questions relatively basic and simple. As time goes on, and she gets more comfortable with you, she would be more apt to share certain information that she was reluctant to in the beginning. Remember, Capricorns aren't secretive, but we are extremely private and will only share information on a need to know basis. Just because we don't have anything to hide doesn't mean you get to know everything. If you have a child you do not support, or are negligent and/or delinquent in handling your financial responsibilities, that will not appeal to Ms. Capricorn. Sure, everyone has a story and we all go through things, but not taking care of your children is a huge red flag that speaks to so many other things about you, none of which are good or even favorable. She is not a "hard nut to crack", with us, sometimes less is more. Don't OD on the texting thing, learn the art of falling back and give her an opportunity to reach out to you (that actually shows, you were on her mind and she is interested in speaking/communicating with you). You may be very attracted to her in every way conceivable, and that's fine, just don't come off too eager or thirsty, because if you do, that could cause her to lose interest and back away. Appearances can be a little deceiving, that's why with Capricorns, I always tell people, don't let the smooth taste fool you.

Some Capricorn women are extremely independent-minded, so much so, that it can cause a problem in potential relationships. Both parties can't be vying for the same role (s), it will never work. I believe roles can and should be clearly defined, understood and respected. There are some Alpha Capricorn females out there, and that coupled with an Alpha male of any sign, is clash city and a recipe for disaster waiting to happen. Her submissiveness in a relationship has more to do with the amount of respect she has for that man who has shown and proven to her that he is more than capable of fulfilling the role as leader of their family with her by his side, every step of the way; Sometimes, her innate sense of independence, coupled with that masculine Saturn energy, will rear its ugly head occasionally, and a clash of wills can ensue. Capricorns are very sensible though; right is right and wrong is wrong. She just wants her feelings and opinions respected. She's not jaded by a long shot, and knows how to voice her opinion or disagreement with something without being condescending, belittling or disrespectful. She wants to be seen and treated as a partner and also being a part of the process, that's all. Capricorn females will be with you throughout whatever, as long as you never cheat on her or betray her trust in a major way, she will be with you and loyal to you until the wheels fall off. Once she has let you inside of her world and/or social circle, you will see firsthand that she is committed to her very small circle of friends. I have always held that, Capricorns may know a lot of people, have some associates, but count very few as actual friends. That said, to her friends, she is normally seen as the rock with which all things can lean in a time of need or turmoil; she is asked and trusted to give great advice because of her detached approach and objective nature. You can literally count on your Capricorn friend to be there with you throughout whatever it is you are going through, to the very end. We are what I call "dog loyal" like that. Not all Capricorn females are objective though, and I don't want to throw a blanket on "all" Capricorns, remember, it depends on the Moon Sign, because some Caps can actually be quite emotional and very subjective, if they possess an emotionally expressive Moon Sign like Cancer or Pisces. Capricorn women just like their male counterparts can be stubborn and unwavering; especially when it comes to something they have already set their sights on and put their plan in motion to. Your approval is not required nor do they seek your validation. They move in a way that best suits them. Win, lose or draw, they take full responsibility. Failure however, is not an option. If we have to reinvent, or tweak some things, so be it; but success never came to anyone who gave up and packed it in, but if you do that, failure will most certainly be at your doorsteps.

THE CHOSEN ONES
CHAPTER 9

Greatness is a given, especially when you're "chosen"; Please excuse our cockiness, and forgive us Capricorns for being able to do whatever, just a little better than you. Kid Rock (Capricorn) came out with a song entitled, "I'm going Platinum", and guess what happened? He went platinum. L.L. Cool J. (Capricorn) said, "Even when I'm bragging, I'm being sincere", LeBron James (Capricorn) has went on record and said that when it's all said and done, he wants to be known as the greatest basketball player that ever lived. Muhammad Ali (Capricorn) said he was the greatest (boxer) and backed up his Capricorn brashness and cockiness with tangible results, i.e. wins and knockouts, and for a long time no-one could beat him. See... proclamations like the aforementioned, mean absolutely nothing, if your action (s) doesn't back them up; Then, it's like, you're just talking because you have lips. Capricorns tend to have an unbending and unwavering faith in our gifts and abilities, and many of us are very vocal about that. R. Kelly (Capricorn) crowned himself the R&B "King", but his string of success in the music industry and over such a long period of time makes that proclamation, not only digestible, but believable. How can you argue that? She's not a "brash", outspoken Capricorn like some others, but Mary J.

Blige is the Queen of R&B/Hip-Hop Soul and her resume backs up that assertion. Again, how can you argue that? You can't hold us, Capricorns were born to stand out, it's something innately embedded in our nature. Remember that legendary group The Temptations? Well, for the longest time, they were the "hitless Temptations", meaning they couldn't score a hit record, that is until a skinny Capricorn guy by the name of David Ruffin joined the group and sung lead on "My Girl" giving them their first certified smash, hit record! He went on to give them a string of other hits too, but he was also a tortured soul, and unfortunately his talent could not save him from his unfortunate destiny. For the record, David Ruffin is the greatest soul singer that ever lived, no-one comes close! (May THE MOST HIGH have mercy on his soul) There's just "something" about us man, Who remembers Dougie Fresh? That song "The Show" was a smash hit, but an unknown rapper that he featured on the B side, performed a song called "La Di Da Di" and ended up not only outshining Dougie Fresh, but went on to sell millions of records and had a better career than Dougie Fresh. That rapper's name is Slick Rick...and he's a Capricorn (January 14, same as mine and L.L.'s) I'm telling you, we don't do well in groups, at least not long term, because we were born to stand out. Even if we start out in a group, we won't stay too long because our nature is such that we have to and will eventually outshine whoever is in the group.

As a rapper, I have been in several groups, and I was always the best one. Now, I know that sounds extremely cocky, but it's the truth, What can I say? Sometimes that can breed jealousy too though; an Emcee knows, group or not, when another Emcee is a better lyricist than they are. Throw in being better looking and if you're not careful you could very well be looking at a Cain and Abel situation. Lyrically, I have never lost a battle, meaning, no rapper who has ever faced me, walked away a winner against me, ever! When I was about 9 years old, out of the clear blue, for reasons I did not know, I started calling myself "The Chosen One", of course being a little rapper, this started out innocently in my raps. As I got older, it made me really reflect on what being "Chosen" really means. I truthfully feel in my heart of hearts that the designation comes from THE MOST HIGH GOD, meaning there are some things we as Capricorns are literally chosen and destined to accomplish. I call them assignments. We aren't chosen because it's some grandiose, over inflated view we have of ourselves, no, many of us were chosen to be a voice for the voiceless, help those who can't help themselves, chosen to make a difference in the lives of others, chosen to awaken a lost people to the truth of who they really are, chosen to use our power and position to effect change, and the list goes on and on. There is a lot of responsibility that comes with being chosen. I found out a little later on in life as I got older that I was a chosen vessel for much of the aforementioned. We are blessed so that we can be a blessing to others. One very admirable trait about Capricorns is our compassion for others and a sincere desire to do what we can to help change the world and make a difference. The Bible says, "For many are called, yet only few are chosen." Which means, there are a small percentage of people walking around the earth who were predestined to accomplish certain things. Martin Luther King Jr. (Capricorn) was chosen, and fulfilled his assignment, Joan of Arc (Capricorn, was chosen, and fulfilled her assignment), what's yours Capricorn? More importantly how close are you to fulfilling whatever it is you were chosen to do? We have to be conscious and cognizant of not turning from "The Chosen One" into The Frozen One, meaning, either being paralyzed with fear and uncertainty, or letting your comfortability breed complacency. Either way, inaction is the result. This is not acceptable. We are held to a higher standard. Grandiose words and proclamations are empty and rhetorical if not backed by actions (s) that produce tangible results. Shouts to many other Capricorns who have made some type of impact on either sports, entertainment, politics or business: *Michelle Obama, Madame CJ Walker, George Foreman, Tiger Woods, Conrad Hilton, Dwayne Wade, Howard Hughes, Eli Manning, Robert Duvall, Dominique Wilkins, Dolly Parton, Bernard Hopkins, Joe Frazier ,Felix Trinidad, Benjamin Franklin, Denzel Washington, Gayle King, Roy Jones Jr. Martin Luther King Jr., Kevin Costner, Elvis Presley, Tyrese, John Singleton, Cuba Gooding, Drew Brees, Edgar Allan Poe, Mary J. Blige, R. Kelly, Anwar Sadat, Kid Rock, L.L. Cool J., Carl Weathers, Slick Rick, Aaliyah, Janis Joplin, Diane Keaton, Steve Harvey, Kirstie Alley*

UNIVERSAL LAWS
CHAPTER 10

There is a Universal Order to things, manifesting one's destiny, speaking things into existence, I'm sure at some point throughout your life; you all have heard these expressions. Is our lives really governed by a set of laws set forth and dictated by the Universe? The resounding answer is yes. First and foremost however, to begin to understand, embrace and unlock the power of The Universe, you have to understand, that GOD is the creator and quarterback if you will, to all happenings within the Universe. You can't give praise to the effect without acknowledging the cause. In Astrology, every single person born into this world has an astrological birth chart; i.e. every single human being is literally aligned with The Universe, and its constellations do have an effect on our behavior and personality traits. The problem is, those who either don't believe what I just said or lack the knowledge and understanding, thereby speaking and having an opinion as someone who is "unlearned", and whatever they say should be taken with a grain of salt anyway. I have always been perplexed about this whole "The Secret" movement that came out some years ago, and felt it was one of the biggest rip-offs ever. Some bright person took a bunch of scriptures from The Bible, and some concepts under Universal Laws, packaged it up, marketed it as a "Secret" and sold millions! I wasn't sold then nor am I impressed now. Having a Business/Marketing Degree, I guess I can't be angry at their marketing strategy, because I understand fully, what the concept of effective marketing entails; marketing is Psychology, knowing how to stimulate others, encourage them to action and get certain reactions based on different types of visual and verbal stimuli. It worked, people sold into it, hook, line and sinker; if I'm not mistaken, I think the author was actually on Oprah; so yeah, it blew up pretty big if "O" had the author on her show. That whole power in spoken word concept came directly from The Bible. As a matter of fact, it specifically states that there is "power of life and death in the tongue" Christ said, whatever it is you desire, believe with your whole heart, have faith the size of a mustard seed, and not only can you move mountains but you will have whatever it is you desire. You can't just rely solely on faith though, there's an action connotation that goes with that, that's why it's called "faith walk". The Bible also says 'faith without works is dead" so there it is there. I can go on and on and line up many of those concepts and Universal Laws taught and pitched as "The Secret", with scripture, but I'm sure you all get the point. When you are spiritually, mentally and physically aligned with the "God Power" of The Universe, That alignment could render you capable of being able to proverbially move mountains. "Contrary to majority belief... Universal Laws are not based on theory or speculation. What at one point was believed to be only theoretical, mystical, or spiritual in nature and understood only by those who learned to tap into the place from where "Higher Truth" comes, has now emerged and become evident in the latest scientific discoveries and is now being measured on a physical level" (Universal Laws, 2012) let's break this down in lay terms. Some of you are probably asking yourself, what is all of this really saying? Please allow me to actually define Universal Laws. "Different from the laws of men, which change continuously depending on circumstances, universal laws are immutable principles that provide the origin and the perfect order of everything in the universe." (Universal Laws, N.D.) There are 7 Major Laws that govern the Universe:

1. Law of Love- States everything culminates from love
2. Law of Manifestation- Says nothing is created, it's either manifested or it's not
3. Law of Polarity- Masculine giver and feminine receiver allows manifestation to take place
4. Law of Evolution- States nothing evolves without first transforming
5. Law of Correspondence- States every situation is a learning experience, every circumstance is generated by oneself...
6. Law of Harmony- Only comprehension prevents destruction
7. Law of Nature- All manifestation in nature requires the right conditions

Now, How is these laws applicable in your life and/or situation? We know that under the law of nature, the right conditions must be present for manifestation to take place; so that long held saying "there's never a right time" isn't true under Universal Law; Our Capricorn nature of waiting and planning for the "perfect time" lines up perfectly with Universal Law, How about that? We also know that The Bible says there is a season, i.e. a time and place for all things. That would actually fall under Universal Order of Creation (just like the masculine and the feminine energy being a natural attraction) The harsh reality is, Sometimes The Universe tells us we have to wait. Clearly THE MOST HIGH knows what we know not. You might think the time is right, and you may even get a little antsy and discouraged because all that you do and have done, it's just not happening for you...Well, that's simply because it's not your season yet, keep moving forward. Keep pressing, keep manifesting...can't stop, will never stop! The only acceptable excuse for a Capricorn giving up is death.

There's a reason it's usually a Capricorn who is the oldest to do something. Our drive, will to win and resiliency is virtually unmatched. We simply will not take no for answer. Resistance is futile, we will win.

CAPRICORN PET PEEVES
CHAPTER 11

I stated earlier, there are a lot of things that tend to annoy Capricorn, But if you want to know what really "gets our goat" (pun intended), I've compiled a nice list of things that will not get you placed on our favorite person list, Capricorns:

1. Do not like people standing over or behind them
2. Do not like repeating themselves
3. Does not want anyone touching their things without asking, doesn't matter who you are
4. Do not like being second guessed or micro-managed
5. Bad breath, if we meet on a first date and I can smell your breath through your face, I promise you there will NOT be a second
6. Find nosey people extremely annoying (mind your business and stay out of everyone else's)
7. Do not show up to their house unannounced, they won't be home...even if they are, they won't be...should have called first (doesn't matter who you are)
8. Are real big on hygiene, do not like bad smells at all
9. Unruly children
10. Do not like people coughing around them in public, even if they make an attempt to cover it (cringe city)
11. Do not like to be goaded, their no means no, leave it alone

12. Find people who refuse to take responsibility for their shortcomings, yet always want to blame others, very annoying

13. Do not like being asked how much something costs

14. Do not truthfully like being told what to do (we want to do what we want, when we want to)

CAPRICORNS AND LOVE MAKING
CHAPTER 12

Capricorns are known to be unselfish lovers who aim to please. Matters of the bedroom are no joke to the goat. Both men and women Caps are known for their stamina, endurance and sexual prowess. You wouldn't know it by their cool, calm, collected exterior, but they are always ready to go a couple rounds. They tend to be extremely passionate with their love making, as with everything else they put their mind and heart to; an inadequate performance in the bedroom is unacceptable to them. I have always held that sex is not everything, or all there is to a relationship, however, it is an important part to the total sum. Fellas, with Capricorn women, if you fall short in this category, literally or figuratively, there is definitely going to be a disconnect in that relationship. Capricorns are not known to be the "freakier" ones of the zodiac, but then again, if you get one with the right moon sign, you could be into something way more than you ever expected. For the majority of us, we put so much time into our job, our business ventures, etc...We don't honestly have a whole lot of extra time for sex, so when we are ready and able to "get it in" we want it to be an extremely enjoyable experience for both parties involved. We understand the responsibility factor in this department once in a committed relationship that goes into this, so we aren't trying to cheat our mate in any way when it comes to sex. The Capricorn woman, on the surface, may seem to some a little uptight, or too conservative, but on the contrary, she is full of fire and passion, just cautious and doesn't readily give that up and away to just any and every one right away. For the most part, she is the consummate "lady in the streets, but freak between the sheets"; so don't get it twisted for one second, the very cool, detached, no-nonsense exterior that's on display to the public gets left on the other side of that door once inside the bedroom with her mate. Again, depending on their moon sign, don't expect anything to over the top in the bedroom from Capricorns on the average. Their conservative natures just doesn't allow for anything too far and above the norm; that said, you may want to get rid of the whips and chains you were hiding in the basement from your last wild relationship. Capricorns are pretty open and aim to please, but they aren't going to get too crazy with it. They are however, very good at what they do. Lovemaking with Capricorn, first and foremost involves having a cozy, comfortable atmosphere with a nice ambiance. They are normally into a lot of kissing, touching, exploration of the body and foreplay that builds up to some really great sex. They love the anticipation, but hate, I mean absolutely hate being disappointed. Take note fellas, don't be bragging, talking about you a Trojan Magnum Man and all that, yet when its time to show and prove, you pull your "thing" out and you come up shorter than a midget on his knees. This wouldn't be good for you homie, keep all the trash talking to a minimal, and save both of you all some potential embarrassment and you not getting another phone call from Lady Capricorn. With Capricorns and sex, it really boils down to whatever they're comfortable with, because bottom line, if they're not comfortable, they're not doing it, and you're just going to have to be mad. This is an eventual conversation you should have in the beginning, ask questions, and its ok to be direct so there is no misunderstanding or communications on what's acceptable to them and what's not. Most Capricorn males are blessed with the ability to delay their own orgasm for as long as need be, just so that they give their partner more than enough time to reach her climax (just to state the obvious, women take longer than men in this area, so you 5 and 10 minute brothers need not apply) They are very unselfish and love pleasuring their mate to uncharted heights of physical ecstasy. Oral sex and Capricorn: believe it or not, in this day and age, some Capricorns are still very conservative in this department and not really open to it, while others see it as a "natural" part of sex, some can take it or leave it, and some even find it repulsive. For the most part, normally, this isn't something they're normally going to engage in casually, because of how intimate it is and how conscious and cautious they are by nature. They tend to reserve this for their committed, monogamous relationships, if they even do it at all, call it what you want, but that's just what it is with them. An actual pre-sex conversation is highly recommended so nothing is assumed and no-one is disappointed. Quiet as its kept, sexual compatibility or incompatibility, depending on which side you're standing on, can literally make or break a relationship. Communication and trust is the top two ingredients for all successful relationships; especially in the beginning stages of getting to know someone. Don't ever assume...talk about it, takes out the guesswork. Capricorns are a lot of things, but mind readers they are not.

COMPREHENSIVE CAPRICORN
CHAPTER 13

"Don't mistake my kindness for weakness. I am kind to everyone, but when someone is unkind to me, weak is not what you are going to remember about me"- Al Capone (Capricorn)

Capricorns are extremely cautious by nature and are definitely not the daredevil, throw caution to the wind types. Sometimes it takes us awhile to try new things because we're really not a big fan of change, especially when we're already used to something or comfortable doing it the way we've been doing it. We tend to be like that with food as well; that said, we have to assess a situation carefully before jumping in head first, you can call it whatever you want, but we want to make sure there is water in the pool before we dive off of the board. Capricorns are the philanthropists of the zodiac, we will help anyone we can without hurting ourselves, and we're one of the most giving, generous and compassionate of people you will ever come across. We'll be a blessing to whomever, but if you take us for granted and are unappreciative, you continuing to get that opportunity falls somewhere between slim and none. Capricorns are fearless by nature, and I don't care how big and "Billy Bad" you think you are, The goats don't run from anyone, and if you really think you want it with one of us, bring it, just be careful what you wish for cause you just might get it. Capricorns like to keep things simple, and pretty much dismiss anything we deem frivolous or non-important, reason being, we hate wasted time and energy, plus silly things and people really annoy us in all honesty. Intelligence rates extremely high with Capricorn, irrespective of your educational background, if you are perceived as not very bright, no disrespect, but that is something that will normally be a turn off and deal breaker for Capricorn. When a Capricorn puts our mind on a goal or mission, almost nothing brings us greater satisfaction than finishing what we started successfully; truly a fulfilling and exhilarating feeling. We tend to live a pretty structured and disciplined life; as such, we normally need to know who, what, when, where, why and how. Impulsiveness is not a trait normally associated with Capricorn. We are the consummate planners. Truthfully, Capricorns are very particular about certain things, like things a certain way, etc... This is why, we unfairly get pegged with "being difficult to live with", actually we aren't, and its real simple; if you respect our privacy, our space and our things? We'll definitely respect yours and there won't be any problems. It's weird, but for Capricorns, we actually pride ourselves on things being in order and having discipline, but at the same time we hate rules, and 9 times out of 10 are annoyed when we have to abide by the ones we deem frivolous. Capricorns do not like people who continuously run their mouth, always having something to say, but the only problem is, they never seem to know what the hell they're talking about. Capricorns never seem to age, I've even heard that we age in reverse; either way, we tend to be blessed with the spirit of youth, especially as we get older, we do tend to look much younger. A "problem" many wish they had right? It's ok to be a little assertive with Capricorn, but not too assertive or aggressive, we do not respond well to aggressiveness at all and have no problems shutting down until you can talk to us like you got some sense.

We aren't in the business of going around making enemies of folk; we are very quiet, unassuming and go about doing whatever we have to do for ourselves and our families. For some reason though, many people, especially in the workplace, find Capricorn's quiet or vocal drive and ambition intimidating. We can truthfully be your best friend or your worst enemy; we'll let you decide which. We actually don't hold grudges, and I know that seems to be the popular sentiment with Capricorn, but I tend to look at it a completely different way; we just never forget what kind of snake you really are and make a conscious effort not to put ourselves in position to be betrayed by you again. Fool us once, shame on you; fool us twice. Oh hell no, it's not 'gonna' happen. Try to tell us we can't do something, and Capricorn will go to our grave trying to prove you wrong, we love people that doubt us and we end up making them look stupid, standing there with egg all over their face. Contrary to popular belief, Capricorns are not driven by money, we are driven by purpose and the idea of success. With certain levels of that comes money, so there it is there. We thrive on balance and stability. If you're all over the place, inconsistent, a big talker and not a doer, you will be a turn off to Capricorn and not a good romantic match at all.   Capricorns are kind of OCD by nature; everything has to look and feel "just right", if something is out of place we'll notice it immediately. If we have paper money in our pockets, the bills have to be placed from the largest denomination to the smallest, anything else would just seem weird to us. We'll notice the smallest piece of lint on someone, and here's the kicker...we won't be ok until that piece of lint is actually gone, 'gotta' love us! When a Capricorn is angry or really irritated, fall back and just give them their space, or risk having your feelings hurt. The comic book character that sums up Capricorn the best is the Incredible Hulk; Dr. Banner is laid back, very intelligent and doesn't bother anybody, but you come messing with him and piss him off....don't make us angry, you wouldn't like us when we're angry. (Capricorn smash!) Capricorns love engaging, thoughtful conversation, but we can't stand chatter boxes, people who just talk and talk but aren't saying anything, annoys us to no end, we'd much rather be doing something way more exciting like, I don't know, watching paint dry maybe? #skin crawl Capricorns only bring a select few into their inner circle and give the title "friend", if you happen to be one of those so chosen, congratulations, you now have someone in your life that will be your friend through thick and thin, even if all others forsake you.

Capricorns and their confidence is normally mistaken for arrogance, while it is true they can be extremely cocky; This trait speaks more to their unwavering belief that they have in themselves, their skills and their abilities. If you ask a Capricorn to borrow money and don't pay it back? You better be like Keith Sweat and ""make it last forever because you won't get another red cent from the goat. Capricorns are very peaceful by nature and try to avoid any type of drama at all costs, but we can become very mean and aggressive, if provoked or pushed past our tolerance level. Be forewarned and antagonize us at your own risk. Contrary to popular belief and opinion, Capricorn is not afraid of taking risks, we understand that risk is a prerequisite of success, but we don't just up and do things with no thought or planning behind it, our risks are calculated. Planning increases the chance of success. It's not 100% guarantee, but we'd much rather plan than just go off halfcocked.

Capricorns are extremely cautious by nature, sometimes overly cautious, to the point where it may cause us to miss out on certain opportunities; Oh well, I guess you can't miss what you never had right? One thing a whole lot of other people can learn from Capricorn, is that if we call you a friend, At a time of crisis or human conflict, You never have to wonder which and who's side we're on...We don't do sleeping with the enemy, and we are what I call "dog loyal" to our close family and friends. Capricorn males are considered the "charmers" of the zodiac, we may not say much when we walk into a room but our presence speaks volumes, because no one in that room is cooler or has their stuff together more than us. Women love the so-called mysteriousness of the goat; here's the thing though, we're not mysterious at all, just cautious and tend to take our time with getting to know someone, same as our Capricorn women. For Capricorn, working hard to achieve material comfort for ourselves and our family is great, having a lot of money in the bank is wonderful, but having a mate you can depend on, unequivocally, and whose loyalty is unquestioned, is priceless. Truthfully, Capricorns tend to build ourselves a bubble, and in that bubble, is our own little world of family and a few close friends; if you fall outside that bubble, here's a few things you need to know, number one, it's not an easy task to get inside of our world, two we mind our business so you really should learn how to mind yours, three we do not care what you think about it or us, and fourth and finally if you have any doubt or skepticism to anything I just said, refer back to number three. If you lie or have told several lies to a Capricorn, but can't remember them? Don't worry, we'll remind you of every single one; our memory is like an elephant. Capricorns can be brutally honest, so if you don't want to hear the un-cut, raw truth, you may not want to ask a Cap. Contrary to popular belief, Capricorns are not pessimistic, we're realists and see things for what they are; sometimes the harsh reality of a situation is just bleak, and for whatever reason, some people have a hard time dealing with that fact; not us, hurt us with the truth, we respect that and will deal with it, whatever it is; but comforting someone with a lie, while it may help temporarily, long term prognosis is not good.

Capricorns will help whoever we can, when we can, that's why when someone is unappreciative, ungrateful, and unthankful or we feel taken for granted it angers us, and will make us rethink the relationship, especially if this behavior is systematic. The intentions of our heart are always good, so when Capricorn does something for someone or reaches out, it's genuine, so for this reason, it bothers or hurts us when our intention is taken for something else. If a Capricorn commits to something or someone, please believe we take pride in all of our commitments, because if we don't want to commit, we just won't; We don't approach anything half way, it's all in or all out with us, no middle ground or grey areas; so it's a given we expect the exact same thing if someone commits to us.

Capricorns are homebodies for the most part, aside from work, that's probably where the majority of Caps spend most of their time, and many of us work from home.....so there it is there. We love the peace, solitude and serenity being at home provides us. I've heard people say Capricorns like to debate, really? That's news to me; maybe a few of us might like to engage in that (depending on their Moon), but for the most part, Caps don't have the patience nor the tolerance to be going back and forth with someone who clearly has no inclination to agree. We speak ours and keep it moving, it's pointless to "argue" and wasted energy is a waste of time. If you tell a Capricorn you're going to do something, we have this weird condition of actually expecting you to do it. Losing faith and accountability with Capricorn is truthfully the beginning of the end. If we could, Capricorn would feed and clothe everyone in need. We have big hearts, and by nature want to make a difference, and try to change the world.

Capricorns are very serious and no nonsense; many use this to say we're unapproachable, unfriendly or anti-social... not true at all. When we're handling business we take that very seriously and don't have time for socializing, playing around, laughing and whatnot, but when the time is right, we're one of the warmest and most engaging you'll ever meet. Truthfully, Capricorns have a rebel spirit; we actually pride ourselves on things being in order and having discipline, but at the same time we don't really like rules, and 9 times out of 10 are irked by it when we have to abide by the ones we think are silly. Capricorns are very fair minded, we don't expect anything from you that we aren't willing to give. Capricorns can be somewhat intimidating with our everybody keep away demeanor and attitude, but if you can make it past our defensive mechanism, you'll see just how amazing we really are. Without an emotionally expressive Moon Sign, Most Capricorns keep feelings and emotions inside; As a matter of fact you wouldn't even know we're hurt unless we straight up tell you we're hurt or something is bothering us. We can't stand pettiness and small mindedness; it's very annoying not to mention a turn off. Capricorns tend to believe in karma, so if you hurt us, do us wrong in any way or betray us, we take a form of solace in knowing that you will get that back, and sometimes 20 times more than what you did to us.

Capricorns work extremely hard to provide nicely for our family, and although we tend to be low key, we do like really nice things, and believe that all hard work should be rewarded, so enjoy all the fruits of your labor, you've earned it Capricorn. Loyalty is everything to a Capricorn, to know and feel in your heart, without a shadow of a doubt, that someone is in your corner, is worth more than all the money in the world. Capricorns do not; I repeat do not like to be goaded or pushed, if we tell you the answer to something, that's what it is, if you continue to try and goad us, trust me, nothing in this world can prepare you for the eruption that will soon follow. Capricorn can, at times, seem to hold the weight of the world on our shoulders, yet many times we feel there isn't anyone like this, there for us. Capricorns hate loose ends, and don't like things hanging over our heads. If we decide to call a relationship or marriage quits, this is not going to be one of them 2, 3, 4 and 5 year "legal" separations, nah, if it's over, let it be over, we want that divorce ASAP so we can move on with our lives and you yours. Capricorn, is not trying to get into your business because we're too focused on our own, something you need to learn to do; we do not like busy bodies, always trying to find out peoples business just so they can gossip like little school girls...it's annoying as all get out. Capricorns have a fighter and protector spirit, we aren't afraid to stand when everyone else would rather sit....no fear...we'll bring it. Capricorns were born to stand out. Rule number one for us, is there is no number two. A huge turn off for Capricorn is people who refuse to take responsibility and accountability for their flaws and shortcomings, blaming everyone else instead of using that energy to become a better person. Capricorns don't normally or often harden our heart towards someone, but if you happen to be on the receiving end, that means we've turned cold towards you; congrats, you have to be some kind of special for that to happen with us (and I do mean "special" sarcastically) and oh, if we harden our hearts towards you, it's a wrap, nothing you can say or do is going to change that. Capricorns do not like whiners and complainers, we have no problem helping you, giving great sound advice, etc..., but if you don't listen and want to continue along your chosen path, go ahead, but don't keep coming to us with the same stuff. At some point you have to suck it up, and do what you have to do to make your situation better. Constantly complaining about it is not going to change it, corrective action does that. Don't ever underestimate the heart, will, drive, resiliency and desire of a Capricorn.

Capricorns are blessed with an array of God given talents, gifts and abilities, and because of this many of us find it difficult to concentrate on just one, but we have to focus Caps, that one will open the door for all our other talents and gifts. Capricorns get very anxious when we have things that need to be done or a project needing to get finished, which is why we hate depending on others to get stuff done. We don't crack under pressure, no matter what. Caps are very creative, and we're always thinking of new ways or starting some new business venture to generate income. A Capricorn's body language will let you know if we're in the mood to socialize, and if you don't get the hint by the," what the hell are you bothering me for?" look on our face, our extremely short answers and lack of engagement should do the trick. Caps tend to have a healthy dose of respect for religion and science; we figure much can be learned from both, and sometimes merging the two can bring clarity to confusion. We take our time with things and will not be forced or rushed into anything by anyone, doesn't matter who you are, what you look like, what your status is, none of that. Capricorns are very classy and tasteful, so a first date doesn't have to cost a lot of money, as long as some thought was put into it; and whatever you do, do not come off "cheap" (Aquarius!) If funds are a little low, you might want to get your dividends up just a little and make sure your Cap has a really good time. Whatever you do, never assume anything with Capricorns. Ladies, if a Capricorn male shows interest, wants to take you out and spend some time with you, don't assume he's doing so because he has an agenda. A Capricorn is not into wasting time and energy, if they express interest, trust me, it's genuine. Fellas, just because a Capricorn female went on a few dates and you spent a couple dollars doesn't mean she's going to just jump in bed with you; it's not that easy or simple. with Capricorns everything takes time, and if we're both attracted to one another in that way, sex will more than likely happen...eventually, but it's not a given, not with us it's not. People are generally taken aback with just how cool and down to earth Capricorns really are. We are some of the best looking and most successful of all in the zodiac. Normally, with these qualities, people tend to think we would be full of ourselves, but nothing could be further from the truth with us; because we know that first of all, "beauty" is truly in the eyes of the beholder, and you need a lot more than that to have and sustain a healthy, happy and successful relationship, bottom line. Capricorns, in all reality are more relationship minded, and yeah we do hate dating, and think the dating scene is a drag, however, we will date, but tend do so more with a purpose, other than just hooking up to have fun, what the hell is that? In all seriousness, we would much rather be with "The One". Image is everything to Capricorn; we do classy, stylish and elegant. Always make sure you have yourself together when going out with one of us because we are definitely going to have our stuff together. And smelling nice is essential. Capricorns thrive on being in control, including our surroundings, our feelings, and our life. If you keep a messy house and call yourself inviting a Capricorn over, I'll save you some trouble...don't! Clean your house first, if not, I guarantee you two things, 1. Capricorn will not be staying long and 2. You will never get another visit from them. You never get a second chance to make a first impression. Sounds cliché, but so very true. Capricorns are known for their courage and fearlessness. They won't avoid an enemy or a person they know doesn't like them because they're afraid, nah, we avoid people like that because we know in our mind and hearts what we're capable of, and we're not trying to go there or get taken there; with us, it's 0 or 60, and a Cap at 60 is pretty damn scary.

Capricorns do tend to have high standards, but we are not hard to please, that's just not true. The exact opposite is actually true for us. If we're into you, all we ask for is respect, honesty, reasonable space and consider our feelings, not just yours. Capricorns possess a trait that's rarely even talked about these days....honor; To the best of our ability we, by nature, are driven to do what's right, even if deep down we don't like it, we can't help it, I love that about us. Capricorns hate to lose, but more than anything we hate to fail, and sometimes depending on what it is, it is extremely difficult for some of us to accept this. Caps have a very keen sense of observation, which is why we don't say much to and around people we don't know; we're taking it all in, seeing who's who and what's what, not too much gets by the "G.O.A.T." though. Capricorns can be extremely persistent when we have our eyes set on a specific goal, almost nerve wrecking like persistence, but we must get it, failure is not an option. Capricorns are not dreamers, we're visionaries; to dream is to fantasize, i.e. not reality, there's an action connotation that goes along with being a visionary and we embrace that emphatically. Capricorns are slow to love, but when we do, we "love hard", but make no mistake, and read this carefully, we do have our limits, and no matter how much we love you, if you continue to disrespect, disregard, disappoint, disappear, disapprove, are disloyal, we won't have to discern, you will be discharged and dismissed. Capricorns normally have no problem thinking outside the box. Sometimes the wheel does have to be reinvented, and we're the masters at that. We rarely let people in on our vision, goal (s) or aspirations, because either they won't understand it, can't see it, or have unsolicited opinions that we really could care less about. We'll show you much better than we can ever tell you. We don't care if you understand or agree with our vision; it's ours, not yours, Comprende? With Capricorns, we never say die, if there's a will there's a way, and we are going to find it, period. Capricorns tend to be very nonjudgmental. Do you and be who you are, if it doesn't "line up" or conflicts with who we are, i.e. you have too many flaws or short comings to our liking? We simply won't deal with you. No harm no foul, compatibility is not just for romantic relationships; it's for two people who desire to be friends as well. In the mist of chaos, when all hell breaks loose, Capricorns can be counted on to be the voice of reason. Capricorns don't care who's doing what or where, we march to the beat of our own drum; and no, really, we don't care; has no bearing whatsoever on what we've got going on. Capricorns are without question, creatures of habit. Once we get comfortable doing something, we will pretty much always stick with it. We truthfully do not like un-solicited advice and find people who seem to always know what you should be doing and how very annoying. We are however, very sensible, reasonable and open to anything that makes sense; sometimes it may take us a little longer to adopt new thinking/new ways of doing things, but trust, if it makes what we're doing better, or easier, we'll switch, just takes us a little while to transition. Capricorns expect nothing less than the best from our family and close friends, because that's exactly what we give. Some people say our standards are too high and we expect too much, which is a bunch of bull, that's just an excuse because you're lazy and we call you on it every time, stop that snickering and bickering, we're not trying to hear that, chop, chop.

Capricorns are very stubborn and can get downright defiant when it comes to doing something we just do not want to do, or someone trying to force us into something we're just not feeling. Once our heels are dug in, you're not forcing Capricorn into anything, so just leave that alone because the only thing you're going to succeed in is making us very angry. Once our minds is made up, it's pretty much a 'done dada', fall back with all that though, seriously. If we have a change of heart or whatever, we'll let you know. Yes, Capricorns by nature are loners; no, we're not anti-social; yes, we know how to laugh and have a good time; no, we have no tolerance for ignorance or foolishness; yes, we are very generous and will give someone our last; no, we are not door mats and will not be used or stepped on; yes we are kind, peaceful and respectful to all; no, we will not be bullied, disrespected or forced into anything; yes, we do have traits and qualities that you will never understand; and that's ok, because we're sure you do as well. Capricorns, by nature need "private time", doesn't matter what our status is (married, dating, living with significant other, etc...) We are subject to go into our own "little world" and don't want to be bothered by anyone for a while. This is just how we "get our mind right" and replenish. Our mates have to really understand this about us and not be offended, take it personally, or eventually this trait would cause problems in our relationships. You can call it "moody" or whatever you like, but this is how we are by nature; you may not understand it, but we simply ask that you respect it. Capricorn will damn near give you the heart out of our body, that's really how kind and generous we are, but with us, it's all about your approach; If you're kind, courteous and respectful we'll respond favorably, but if you come at us in a foul way or real domineering/demanding, The only thing you better get, Is out of our face with all that; Like my mom used to always says," you ain't the two and we ain't the one". If a Football Team was put together comprised of the Zodiac, Capricorn would be the quarterback; because we're natural born leaders, cool under pressure, hard to pin down, we're normally the smartest on the field and can score at will. Handling yourself with class and dignity, especially in public, with Capricorn is an absolute must. We hate to be embarrassed and for someone to bring unnecessary attention to us by making a scene, being loud, and obnoxious. Huge no no, could or would be your first and last time out with Capricorn. Caps are real big on justice, so it goes without saying, we despise injustice; when someone hurts us really badly or does us wrong without just cause, some of us can become really consumed with that energy, and either harbor hate or vengeance, to the point of us even dreaming about it. We really take stuff like that to heart, but, we have to learn the art of "letting go" Caps, Karma will take care of that person or those people, guaranteed. You wouldn't know this by how self-assured and confident many Capricorns come across, but we are actually our own harshest critics; Tend to get angry with ourselves for making even the most simple of mistakes, that 9 times out of 10 we felt was avoidable. That's just the perfectionist side to our nature, but also why we hate to be criticized, because we feel we get enough of that on our own, with no help from anyone else. Internally we're like, how the hell didn't I know or catch that?! *Instant attitude* Capricorns have no problem admitting when we're wrong, it just so happens we're not wrong a lot, Seriously, the two words we hear the most are: "you're right"; For some reason, people hate that and try to hate on this quality/trait we possess, But hey, don't blame us, it is what it is. In the face of extreme adversity and what looks like insurmountable odds, Capricorn takes a deep breath, meet whatever head on, continue moving forward and eventually overcome whatever adversity we're facing, That's how GOD made us. If a Capricorn tells you they are going to do something, you can depend on them to get that done. And if for whatever reason, circumstance changes beyond our control and we can't, we're considerate, respectful, mindful and will let you know that (beforehand), not simply leave you hanging or not do what we said. If a Capricorn shares something with you that could be deemed personal or private, they aren`t seeking any type of validation from you, input, advice, nor are they trying to impress you with anything, that means they are comfortable with and trust they can be open and honest with you; Don`t make them regret that, because once a Capricorn shuts down, an act of Congress can`t get them to open back up. Capricorns do not believe in giving up, especially when we have goals set and a strong belief in ourselves and our abilities along with the drive, will and resilience to accomplish them; One of our traits is knowing when to reinvent ourselves, i.e. change some things up or switch some things around, all in the spirit of accomplishing our set goals. We are the masters of reinvention. Whoever coined the phrase "more than one way to skin a cat" was either a Capricorn or had one in mind. Capricorns by nature are very generous. They will think nothing about helping out a loved one financially, but the flip side is, Most Caps don't know how to accept or even ask for help from anyone, which is weird given how willing they are to help others. This is why many Caps will "suffer in silence" before they ask anyone for help. I think this trait comes from Capricorns not ever wanting to appear "needy", weak or incapable. Sidebar: There is nothing "weak" about needing help, and when you have consistently helped others, this scriptural concept is called "sowing seeds"; when you sow seeds, eventually you reap a harvest. It doesn't make sense for you to plant seeds, then refuse to eat from the harvest it brings forth.

Capricorns aren't normally rude, but they can be extremely shrewd and matter of fact; especially when it comes to business. They have the best poker face in the game and when it's time to get down to business, This sign does not have time to be 'skinnin and grinnin' with you, not when there's work to be done. Capricorn does not like to be rushed. We like to take our own sweet time with stuff. Weird part about that is that we will sometimes wait until the last minute to get stuff done, and yeah, we're in a race against the clock, but we actually get a "rush" off of that (no pun intended) That's just the complex nature of the goat, don't ask. Capricorns are not pessimists; we just don't do the whole rose colored glasses thing, Sorry. Many find Capricorn intimidating in the work place because of our ability, quiet and sometimes vocal ambition to move to the "top", and our sometimes not so subtle attitude that we are really the best qualified. Taking orders from those we feel are less qualified or capable is a driving force as well. Capricorns are normally blessed with great intuition and natural insight, called the spirit of discernment. That gift allows them to see right past a lot of BS, so don't even think about. Quietly and sometimes vocally, Capricorns are normally ambitious and desire to ascend to the very top of the mountain in their respective fields and genres. A Capricorn will rarely tire of their own company. Capricorns can be the consummate "work-a-holics", and it seems like there's always something to do with us, but make no mistake, we do know how to break away and make time for ourselves and/or our significant others because we realize there is a level of responsibility that comes with our committed relationships. Capricorns are normally objective by nature. Their ability to stand back from a situation and assess it based on reason and logic, instead of emotion, makes them ideal for leadership/management positions. A Capricorn will never settle for less than what they deserve or have worked extremely hard for. We have been known to sit things out, until the result fits our goal (s), dream (s) or aspiration (s)...By nature, we're just not real big on settling. Capricorns are respectful of everyone until or unless they are disrespected or treated differently. Normally, we don't care about your social or economic status; our general outlook is that all human beings deserve a measure of respect.

CAPRICORNS- THE DARK SIDE
CHAPTER 14

I would be remiss in my duties as the creator and administrator of the biggest, most accurate and comprehensive Capricorn Community in the world, and this book could hardly be considered "comprehensive" if I only gave all the great and wonderful qualities and behavioral traits that Capricorns possess. If nothing else, Capricorns are known to "keep it real", even if it hurts or stings a little in the process. Capricorns can be extremely intolerant and dismissive. If we deem it frivolous, we'll simply ignore it, wave it off and not give it any energy whatsoever. Our extreme confidence in our skills and abilities are often taken for arrogance; some of us are quite vocal about it, while other Caps want to silently crush all competition into the ground with a proverbial "foot wedgy" to the side of the forehead. For some reason, people generally don't have a problem with someone's excellence or "greatness", only when that "someone" is actually vocal about it (as some Capricorns are, see Muhammad Ali and LeBron James) is when people have the problem or issue, with a proclamation of greatness. Things that make you go hmmmm. Many take Capricorn as too uptight and need to "loosen up". You all must understand this though, with Capricorn, how we are viewed and taken is of the utmost importance to us; that said, we understand there is a time and place for all things. If we're focused on a task at hand, we're not going to be as footloose and fancy free, because that, in our mind, tends to take away focus, and focus is most definitely the name of our game. When the time is right, Capricorn does know how to unwind, laugh, have a good time and be silly even, but they will not be taken lightly or taken as some sort of joke by anyone. We carry ourselves in the most respectable manner at all times regardless of environment, and trust, people do take notice of that; because of our aloof or detached nature, many people take this to mean that we think we're better than others, superior, elitist or snobby. Again, I'm glad I wrote this book, because you all will see that you had Capricorn pegged wrong. We aren't any of the aforementioned, but I can see how that could be perceived in that way; we're truthfully just very no nonsense, and don't have time for silliness and things that are time wasters and non-productive. For example, if you need or want to ask Capricorn for something, and you're taking too long to get to the point, we may very well say, "Hey can you get to the point, I kind of have some other things I need to go and do" or something along those lines. Now, some may call that rude, but with us, we simply prefer you to get right to the point. There's no need to take us all around the world, say what it is you want or need, we can respond, then both of us can continue on with our day. Save the long, drawn out stories, it's not necessary with us. You wouldn't think this would be considered a "bad" trait, but sometimes our ambitious nature is seen as just that .When was it ever a crime to want to live up to your potential and live a life, you are more than capable of living? So, wanting more for yourself and your family, especially when you have the talent, drive and determination to achieve it is a "bad thing"? O.K., let me step outside of my Capricorn Shell for a minute and try to give this notion some type of context. Truthfully, some Capricorns are not simply ambitious, but some can be ruthlessly ambitious; i.e. will step on whoever, do whatever they have to do, to get to the top of that proverbial mountain. I will concede, there is a negative connotation attached to anyone "ruthlessly" trying to obtain something. Rather it's a position, status, to gain an advantage over others, etc...I will concede that, and in that regard, I can see how ruthless ambition could be considered a negative trait. To our credit collectively however, I do have to add, that not all Capricorns are wired this way (as I always say, you better check their moon sign). The absolute biggest "knock" I get against Capricorns is our "Cold" or detached nature. Yes, without an emotionally expressive Moon Sign, Capricorns for the most part are very detached emotionally and not prone to letting others into their feelings and definitely not letting their guard down into matters of their heart. Majority of Capricorns view showing feelings or emotions as "weak", and they never want to appear weak, and seem vulnerable or incapable. Capricorn's pride is also ferocious, and why many would actually rather "suffer in silence" than to break down and ask anyone for help. My Moon Sign is Cancer, so this Capricorn is very expressive with what I'm thinking, how I'm feeling, etc... We are known to be very stubborn, but this doesn't mean nor am I trying to imply that we are uncompromising. At the end of the day, we move in a way that's most suitable for us, our thoughts, views, ideologies, etc....We are the masters of ourselves, and win, lose or draw, we can live with the results, because in the end, we would have done it our way. No one to point a finger at, we take full responsibility.

Capricorns are actually very reasonable and open to anything that makes sense; two things will determine if they will consider what's being presented to them. 1. The way it is presented and 2. Do they deem it credible and/or believable; it's really as simple as that. They can appreciate good, sound, intelligent input that makes sense, but ultimately, it has to make sense to them; win, lose or draw. A couple other negative adjectives used to describe Capricorns are distrusting, conceited, demanding, controlling, pessimistic and introverted. Ok, so let's deal with it. I personally don't understand how anyone could view being distrusting as a negative. Let's not act like there aren't bad people out there who have hidden agendas and ulterior motives that may very well involve you being on the receiving end of the agenda in a negative way. I see nothing wrong having someone prove themselves and what they're about (by their actions) thereby earning your trust, vice giving it to them unconditionally and leaving yourself open and susceptible to whatever. I don't think that's very smart at all. Conceited? Nah, again, I think people sometimes confuse our confidence in ourselves as arrogant or being conceited, the reality is, in spite of our occasional cockiness and brashness, we are subject to display at times, and we are actually quite humble. Some might say, well how can you be cocky and humble at the same time? My reply is this: it's one of the nuances that explain the complex nature of being born under the zodiac sign of Capricorn. Pessimistic, Hardly, We pride ourselves in being realists. Major difference and many don't seem to know the difference. Some people simply can't deal with the harsh reality of some situations. Capricorns will simply and honestly tell it like it is. We're going to give you an open and honest assessment; you have two choices, you can deal with it or not. Controlling? The only thing we are controlling about, is our behavior and our environment. This is a false accusation. I will concede that some of us only trust our assessment and decision making, in which, that can come off or appear as controlling; but looked at a little closer, it's simply someone who wants to "get it right" by going with what they are most comfortable with. Introverted? Ok, you got us there, but since when is not being very sociable a crime? I mean, we can be sociable if we so desire. Truthfully, Capricorns are normally very funny and can literally be the life of a party, provided they are comfortable in the environment. Since we were children, Capricorns are used to spending a lot of time alone, in their own thoughts, entertaining themselves. That's just how we are by nature. We are at our most comfortable when we're doing something we really enjoy or that interests us. I take exception with domineering, because that implies that we are somehow bullies that ride rough shod over others, and that is definitely not true or indicative of anyone born under the sign of Capricorn. We have no problem leading and/or taking control, especially if there is some hesitation or trepidation in doing so, on the part of anyone we are involved with either personally or professionally. Again, with Capricorn, you have to show and prove to us that you are equipped and/or qualified to carry out whatever task, or assume the responsibilities for whatever position you have either professed or made a commitment to. We're just not into putting our life (literally or figuratively) in the hands of someone else who has not shown they are worthy of such a responsibility and designation. Much of what people consider a "dark side" is really simply a misunderstanding of how we operate, how we approach things and what goes into our thought process.

CAPRICORNS IN BUSINESS
CHAPTER 15

I spoke about how, even in the mist of chaos, Capricorn can be counted on to be the voice of reason, and make sound decisions based on reason and logic, not emotions. We are also fair minded, tend to speak with the spirit of wisdom, plus have a great deal of common sense. All of these are excellent leadership traits, especially if you desire to go into business for yourself and become an entrepreneur. Capricorns like the freedom of being able to do what they want to do, when they want to do it. Naturally, going into business for themselves is something that is very appealing to them. They were born to lead, and with good, sound judgement have all the personality prerequisites for success on any level. When it comes to business, Capricorns can be extremely shrewd, hardnosed and tough. They are the consummate visionaries and tend to lead with an acumen for detail, and a clear cut understanding of what the ultimate goal and mission is, and not lose sight or focus. They make excellent CEO's because they have a natural, keen understanding and insight as to what motivates individuals and how best to maximize everyone's potential. Infinite potential is pointless if you don't know how to tap into your inner self and pull out greatness. Our symbol is interchanged between sea goat (a mythical animal) and a mountain goat (a real animal) the sea goat is known to have a fish tail, that fish tail is supposed to represent sensitivity in Capricorn. Mountain Goats are slow and methodical, but their goal is to get to the top of that mountain. They may stop and survey things along the way, makes some adjustments, etc...but they keep on plodding and moving forward up that mountain. Slowly at times, but steady nonetheless. Eventually, they will get to the top of the mountain. That's me all the way! I identify wholeheartedly as the mountain goat; not only that, but I also tend to be non-fictitious by nature, meaning I can't and don't really identify with anything if it's not based on reality; the sea goat is not real, as such, I do not and cannot identify with it.

With Capricorns, when it comes to business, the gender is irrespective. Capricorn women are just as shrewd and no-nonsense as the men. If you think you're going to simply run over her in the boardroom, think again. One of the things we hang our hat on with respect to success and failure, is preparation. We're not going to come off halfcocked or without having done our due diligence. This is why when we speak on something, we tend to speak with great confidence and authority because we've already armed ourselves with every conceivable amount of information necessary to get our point across and close the deal. Capricorns also make great lawyers, public speakers, teachers and professors (many having a passion for teaching, and teaching is without question one of mine) Above all else, we pride ourselves in making good, sound decisions. Another huge misconception about Capricorn is that we are afraid to take risks. This simply is not true. I will admit, that yes, we are extremely cautious by nature, but we do understand that there is a level of risk involved that is sometimes uncomfortably wed with success; as such, our risks are more calculated, meaning, again, we've done our due diligence, weighed all the pros and cons, etc...We typically don't make rash decisions on any level, not just in business, but our personal lives as well. All we do is win, losing is never even thought of as an option and 2nd place is unfathomable. Capricorn's never say die, where there's a will, there's a way attitude and outlook on life, coupled with their relentless persistence makes for a formidable business person. Normally, a Capricorn's business and entrepreneurial aspirations, starts with the desire, first and foremost to be their own boss, make their own rules, manifest their own destiny and be in complete control of their own lives. We are determined, good organizers and extremely responsible. Success is relative, and dependent upon what an individual views success as; for some it's based on money or net worth, while for others it's based on one's contentment in life, their family is good, healthy, etc...and me, I view success as living life by your own rules. If you can get up in the mornings when you desire, take a vacation when you want, and not be financially dependent on anything or anyone for your economic existence? Then you, by my definition and terms are successful. Capricorns are not "money hungry" and we unfairly get accused of being very materialistic. We don't worship money, and money is most certainly not our God. We truly desire to make a change and or difference in the world, or at the very least, in the lives of others; understanding that when God blesses you financially, He does so, so you can in turn, be a blessing to others; not be selfish, greedy and not use your position of power and wealth to help make an actual difference, not a symbolic, empty gesture of making a donation, then going about the rest of your day. No one is more aware of this than Capricorn. It is not lost on us that money allows you certain opportunities that are tangible and can have a huge, positive impact on the lives of others.

CAPRICORNS AND THE SPIRIT OF YOUTH
CHAPTER 16

They never seem to age, and it has even been said that Capricorns tend to "age in reverse"; meaning, while young they look older and when they're older they look younger. I don't know about all that, but I do know that at a young age, Capricorns are normally very wise, especially in comparison to other children in the same age bracket. Actually, it's pretty difficult to determine how old or how young a Capricorn is, because of how they speak when they're younger and how they look once older. Truthfully, it's all just the same to us because we'd much rather not be put in a box or pigeon-holed by anyone. No matter where you are in life or what you do, you're always going to be "too" something to someone. Rather it's too old, too young, too inexperienced, too needy, too skinny, too fat, etc...etc...People in general, incorrectly, consciously and sometimes sub-consciously look for ways to exclude. Why this is done can be debated from a psychological standpoint in another forum, but for the purpose of this book, I'm going to stay on the surface with this particular subject. Jealousy is one of the oldest spirits in existence. It actually gave us the first recorded murder in history with Cain killing Abel, Why? Look no further than the spirit of jealousy. Now, if you don't believe In God or believe in the bible, again, that's fine. Still doesn't take away from the operative I'm bringing forth, which is jealousy. Ordinarily, when you are gifted and talented enough to do several things that many people are not blessed with the ability to do, many will love and appreciate you for those talents, gifts and abilities. And some will be jealous because of them. That is the harsh yet simple reality of life. Everyone is not going to love and appreciate you; as a result, they consciously or subconsciously look for ways to discourage, discredit or exclude you, your gifts and abilities. This is why it is extremely important not to give way to this type of energy, no matter who or where it's coming from. Capricorns are the masters at drowning out the noise, avoiding the dream killers, and those who seem to always doubt everything yet they have nothing. Your dreams are just that...yours. You don't need permission or validation from anyone to have a dream, and you most certainly don't owe anyone an explanation for pursuing your dreams and goals with an unwavering belief in yourself and your God given abilities. George Foreman was terrorizing the heavyweight division in the 70's, until he met a man by the name of Muhammad Ali in Zaire Africa, for the heavyweight championship in 1973. After that fight and loss, George was never the same. He ended up retiring and eventually going into ministry. Fast forward to the 90's when Foreman came back to boxing and said his goal was to actually fight Mike Tyson and regain the heavyweight championship he lost to Ali way back in 1973. People laughed at him, said he was too old, crazy and delusional. Is that right? Well, guess what, he blocked out all the naysayers and all the noise, and on November 5th, 1994, at 45 years of age, George Foreman knocked out Michael Moorer to become the oldest heavyweight champion ever! and he did so, some 20 years after losing it to Muhammad Ali (Capricorn). And it is no accident that George Foreman, ladies and gentleman is a Capricorn. Ditto with Bernard Hopkins, who at the age of 46, broke George Foreman's record to become the oldest fighter ever to win a championship when he defeated Jean Pascal on May 21, 2011, and yes, Bernard Hopkins is also a Capricorn! That's just how we are designed people, we don't listen to anyone. We do us and don't care about all the unnecessary noise in the background. We have a belief in ourselves, our talents and abilities like nobody's business. We will not relent or continue to pursue greatness, simply because someone says we shouldn't or claim we're too this or too that. When you have something of value to submit to The Universe, bring it forth, no hesitation or second guessing at all. There is no statute of limitation on success. The doubters and naysayers can hear and read about it later. In the mean and between time, you continue to move forward, manifest your destiny, don't take no for an answer and let that one talent of yours open the door for all the others. This is where we as Capricorns run into a little trouble; because our interests, talents and abilities are many, it is often difficult to narrow it down and focus on just one. The old proverb says, 'The hunter who chases two rabbits, ends up catching neither". Don't fall victim to this, your gifts can and will make room for you, but you have to narrow it down and focus on mastering, perfecting and being successful with one; the others will come in due time.

Dr. Manifest

DECEMBER-JANUARY CAPRICORNS
CHAPTER 17

What's the difference?

I spoke earlier at the beginning of this book, and touched on throughout, about how and why it was so important to know yours and your mate's moon sign. Your moon sign in astrology is considered the emotional part of our astrological makeup. In other words, your moon sign gives you the traits that make you respond to things and or people and situations emotionally or more detached (depending on what it is). That alone allows for people born of the same exact sign to be, in some cases, completely different. However, there is something else in Astrology that contributes to us all being Capricorns, yet very different with respect to some of our traits and behavior patterns. In Astrology, it's called the Decan. (told you all astrology isn't as simple as you might think with respect to the behavioral science power it possesses.) The Decan is defined as follows: "Each sign is divided into three divisions of 10 degrees, each sign has 3 Decans, one for each division of 10 degrees. Each decan has a ruler which becomes the sub ruler of the sign or the co-ruler of that sign. Once you are familiar with the Triplicities (fire, earth, air, water), it will be easier for you to determine the sub-rulers of each decan." (Decans in Astrology, 2011) I have gotten this question, probably more than any other question. "Is there a difference between December Capricorns and January ones?" The answer is yes, not drastic differences, but depending on which Decan each Capricorn falls under, the differences are there. Here is a breakdown of the 3 Capricorn Decans:

"If you were born between December 22 and January 1:

This is the first of the Capricorn Decans and is characterized by patience, determination and hard work.

Capricorns are always hard working but this applies even more so to the first of the Capricorn Decans. You also have the determination, strength and will to complete any worthwhile project.

You have tremendous patience but this is tested by 'airy fairy' people who have their head in the clouds and have fanciful ideas. This is because you cannot relate to them as you are well grounded with your feet firmly on the ground. You like to get the job done, rather than dreaming about it.

You are extremely loyal and devoted to those you love and will strive to provide material wealth and security for them. Material wealth is important to you as it firstly shows others how successful you are and thus commands their respect. You value the respect from others, rather than their affection or love. Material wealth also allows you to spoil those you hold dear.

You have the potential to be in careers that allow you to be very successful and powerful. You can be very competitive in the workplace and with your dogged determination will never lose sight of the prize.

The main flaw in this first Decan, are that you can be the victim of low moods, depression or mood swings.

If you were born between January 2 and January 11:

This is the second of the Capricorn Decans and is characterized by charm, creativity and adaptable.

Of all the Capricorn Decans you are by far the most charming and sociable. You collect a lot of good friends throughout your life, as they like your company.

Your creative skills are many and you can create great success for yourself by using them wisely. Your relentless ambition combined with your hard work will allow you to climb to very top of any profession you choose – so long as it uses your creativity.

You take the view that if a job is worth doing, it's worth doing well. This applies not just to your career path but also to your friendships and love relationships. You cultivate and maintain your relationships with 100% loyalty, attention and affection.

The main flaw in this second Decan Capricorn personality is pessimism. Your pessimistic streak can sometimes overtake you and can lead to low moods.

If you were born between January 12 and January 20:

This is the third of the Capricorn Decans and is characterized by intelligence, loyalty and discipline.

You like your world to be ordered, structured and disciplined. You have little time for fanciful notions and abstract concepts. Although you do enjoy the finer things in life and admire beautiful things, you need them to have a practical and functional use as well.

Of all the Capricorn Decans you are the most intelligent and if you are able to override your innate shyness can become a gifted communicator.

Your intelligence coupled with your desire to accomplish makes you ideally suited to careers that demand shrewdness and attention to detail. The Legal profession, law enforcement and teaching are all areas that you can excel in.

You are tremendously loyal and faithful in all your relationships. Once you have placed your trust in someone and allowed them into your life you will fully commit to them.

The main flaw in this third Decan Capricorn personality is a tendency to dwell on the past and hold grudges." (Capricorn Star Sign, 2015)

PERSONALITY CATCHPHRASES FOR ALL 12 SIGNS
CHAPTER 18

Aries- "I don't want wait, I want it, and want it right now! (speaks to their impatient nature)

Taurus- "I'm not doing it, you didn't hear me the first 5 times?" (speaks to their stubborn nature)

Gemini- "Hope you got some time because I can talk for hours" (speaks to their talkative nature)

Cancer- "You hurt my feelings" (speaks to their sensitive nature)

Leo- "I'll do what I want, when I want, with who I want" (speaks to their arrogant nature)

Virgo- "I'm the most awesomest, fantabulous person I know, and you? You aiiiight!" (speaks to their self-absorbed nature)

Libra- "I think I do, no wait, I don't, oh hell, I don't know" (speaks to their indecisive nature)

Scorpio- "What's mine is mine, don't get cut" (speaks to their jealous and possessive nature)

Sagittarius- "Loved by few, Hated by Many, Oh well" (speaks to their carefree nature)

Capricorn- "Don't get mad because I'm better at it than you" (speaks to the cockiness in their nature)

Aquarius- "I don't pay full price for nothing, I got the hook up" (speaks to their frugal nature)

Pisces- "I hope you can read minds cause I 'ain't' telling you nothing" (speaks to their secretive nature)

THE POWER OF SPOKEN WORD
CHAPTER 19

Life does not imitate art. As such, we have to be extremely careful with what type of energy we speak and put into the Universe. The Universe doesn't care about entertainment or creativity and makes no distinction! Here's a list of people and situations that illustrate the point of this segment:

Proverbs 18:21
"Death and life are in the power of the tongue"

1. For years, on television, on the T.V. Show Sanford and Son, Actor Red Foxx faked a heart attack and proclaimed "Elizabeth, I'm coming to join ya honey"...He died in real life from a Heart Attack
2. Ex lead singer of the group H-Town, Keven Conner, in their video called "Emotions" He was allegedly involved in some terrible accident and they didn't know if he was going to make it; they said they were fighting to save him, and never said what type of accident it was nor rather or not he survived, the video said "To be continued..." A couple years later, Keven "Dino" Conner died in a car accident
3. Eminem's best friend "Proof", in the last video he appeared in was ironically a "diss" song aimed at Ray Benzino called "Toy Soldiers", well in the video, Proof gets gunned down and dies, not long after the video, in real life, Proof got gunned down and died
4. Tupac one of the greatest rappers that ever lived, for years made songs like, he sees " death around the corner", "how long with they mourn me", "cradle to the grave", "Life goes on", clearly totally fixated on his own death...Tupac Amaru Shakur was gunned down in Las Vegas, He was only 25

years old

5. Notorious B.I.G.- Much like his mentor Tupac, Biggie burst on the scene, with what many calls an instant classic, proclaiming that he was "Ready To Die", still not having his fill on that, his very next album was entitled 'life after Death"...The Notorious B.I.G. was not long after gunned down as well, and died

Be careful of what you speak out of your mouth, even when "just joking"; and be very careful what you "imitate" or act out in real life, again, again, the Universe doesn't distinguish between what's "art" or what's real; This particular chapter will put a different light on a lot of things, I'm sure, but at least it will make you stop, think and re-evaluate some things. The choice is yours.

COMPATIBILITY ASSESSMENT
CHAPTER 20

This is the age old question. Who is Capricorn most compatible with, who are they least compatible with? Is Capricorn compatible with a Leo, is Capricorn compatible with a Scorpio and the list goes on and on. Before I get into that, I have to give some subtext to the context of what compatibility truly means and just how difficult it is to find a mate who is suitable for you. So let me start here; Scripture tells us that a man and woman must be "equally yoked" in order for a marriage/relationship to work; then it poses the question, "Can two walk together cept they agree'? Equally yoked means, that in pretty much every conceivable category, you two are "made" for one another, i.e. will have pretty much the same ideologies, be compatible sexually, have the same beliefs, will be of the same faith (a Hebrew Israelite and a Muslim, off top renders the two unequally yoked, Just like a Christian trying to marry a Buddhist or something like that) likes, dislikes, etc...And of course the answer to the latter is no, two cannot be in a healthy, happy and harmonious relationship if they are opposite in everything and therefore not equally yoked. The real problem lies in actually finding this person vice thinking you have found them, only to find out after you've contributed and lost time that you're actually not compatible with them after all. Compatibility, like human behavior is extremely complex, and I want to cover this clearly so that you all can get on the same page with me in understanding that. Truthfully, the behavioral science power of the zodiac is a very helpful and useful tool in helping to understand who is most and least likely to be compatible with you. However, if God ordains someone for you, it really wouldn't matter what their sign is, because if God is truly involved and sent that person to you, you will know, because that is the person who is most suitable for you. He knows our likes, dislikes, what turns us on, what turns us off, what we can deal with, what we can't, etc....The real problem is, we don't wait on him, we end up doing it ourselves and 9 times out of 10 end up falling flat on our faces in failed relationship after failed relationship. o.k, let's get back. At the very least, if you are going to try and use the power of the zodiac to help determine compatibility, you have to, at least know that person's Moon Sign as well; yes, there goes that Moon Sign thing again, and it's because In Astrology, your Sun Sign (which everyone pretty much knows, determined by the day and month of your birth) and your Moon Sign (determined by your exact time of birth into the Universe) go together like air and water. In a real generic sense, your Sun Sign represents only 50% of your personality traits and whatever your Moon Sign is, is the other 50%; so if you're judging someone solely on their Sun Sign, you are doing them and yourself a huge disservice because, you're making an incorrect assumption and assessment, only knowing half the story of who they are. Follow me? If you had a bad experience with a Cancer for example, you can't now swear off all Cancers based on the one or two you had bad experiences with, because the traits they possessed, that didn't work for you probably had nothing to do with their Cancer traits (or Sun Sign) and may have had everything to do with whatever their Moon Sign is, This is why, at the very least knowing a person's Moon Sign is so important. Unless you are really deeply, heavily into Astrology and desire to run yours or someone's whole Astrological Birth Chart for reading and assessment purposes, finding out their Moon Sign needs to be done at the very least. Truthfully, when someone is born, their Astrological Chart has 12 positions or houses, and each sign in those positions represent something to your personality and astrological/Universal makeup, but again, if you don't desire to get that deep, at least know the Moon Sign. I could make the argument that knowing the Rising Sign and Venus Sign (in astrology it's called the love house) is just as important as the sun and moon signs with respect to temperament, our approach and how we respond in relationships, hence the "love house". If you desire to run yours or another person's full astrological birth chart, the link is provided below.

http://astrology.about.com/library/bl_freeAstrochart.htm

CAPRICORN-ARIES COMPATIBILITY
CHAPTER 21

For the majority of you Capricorns reading this, and have been in unsuccessful relationships with an Aries, I'm going to go ahead and state the obvious. On any level, Capricorn and Aries is an extremely challenging and difficult combination. For several reasons. Both signs are surrounded by a lot of masculine, alpha male type energy if you will, so just that mere fact alone allows for a lot of potential clashes, disagreements and arguments. In a relationship, both can't play the role of alpha-male. If you remember, earlier in the book I discussed Universal Law right? Well The universal order of things is masculine/feminine, and feminine does not mean weak or subservient at all. It simply means, for there to be a balance in any relationship, both parties have to play their respective roles. All Kings have or need a Queen, sitting side by side with him, sharing in his rulership; there is no shame or dishonor in a woman playing her role as queen, i.e. helping her king lead. That is the basic framework for the compatibility problems of Capricorn and Aries; that coupled with the fact that Aries is the fighter of the zodiac, love to push people's buttons, loves and will never back down from a confrontation, fight (verbal or physical) or argument. (Rosie O'Donnell is the prototype for Aries). Capricorns will not be bullied by anyone, doesn't matter what your sign is or how "Billy Bad" you think you are. You huffing, puffing and beating your chest means absolutely nothing to us. I mean nada, zero, zilch. You're wasting a bunch of air for nothing because we simply are not impressed, afraid or "shook". Our mantra is this, if you really want it, bring it, but be careful what you wish for because you just might get it. Aries impatient and high strung temperament does not, nor will ever work for Capricorn. Capricorns aren't real big on being impulsive, we are planners, and pretty much have to allot and plan for certain things. We tend to be very disciplined and structured, Aries on the other hand is more of the "let's just do it" mind set, and gets really irritated at Capricorn because we look at them like they just touched down from outer space somewhere. Did you all know the relationship between Aries and Capricorn is so strong, difficult and fiery that they even had a huge, knockdown, drag out fight in guess where of all places? *wait for it*.... The Bible! Yes, in The Book of Daniel Chapter 8, The goat (Capricorn) and the ram (Aries) had a classic battle. To save many of you the trouble of having to break out your Bible or Google what I just shared, I'll copy and paste the highlights of their classic battle:

The Book of Daniel
Chapter 8

3 *Then I lifted up mine eyes, and saw, and, behold, there stood before the river a ram which had two horns: and the two horns were high; but one was higher than the other, and the higher came up last.*

4 *I saw the ram pushing westward, and northward, and southward; so that no beasts might stand before him, neither was there any that could deliver out of his hand; but he did according to his will, and became great.*

5 *And as I was considering, behold, an he goat came from the west on the face of the whole earth, and touched not the ground: and the goat had a notable horn between his eyes.*

6 *And he came to the ram that had two horns, which I had seen standing before the river, and ran unto him in the fury of his power.*

7 *And I saw him come close unto the ram, and he was moved with choler against him, and smote the ram, and brake his two horns: and there was no power in the ram to stand before him,*

but he cast him down to the ground, and stamped upon him:
and there was none that could deliver the ram out of his hand.

So yes, the ram lost mightily to the goat! Moral to that, all you Aries, it doesn't matter how much bigger your horns are or how much air you huff and puff, none of that is a match for the goat! The bottom line is this, the difficulty with these two signs is very real, and our contrary natures are even recorded in The Bible of all places. Now, I know there will be a few out there who will say how you've been with an Aries for this amount of time and all that, and that's fine; but I guarantee you your arguments have been one for the ages. I will concede that normally, Capricorn's best sex matches are going to be the fire signs because of both our intense natures and how much we put into love making; the thing is, will the arguments and constant clashing subside long enough to even make it to the bedroom. Doesn't even matter what an Aries Moon Sign is, they are a very difficult match, generally speaking, for Capricorn. Aries is more than a handful, and more than what Capricorn is willing to put up with after a while. I have interviews of Capricorn and Aries couples who have admitted to some of their clashes literally being violent, i,e, physical. No surprise there; so if you make a conscious decision to get into a what you think is a long term relationship with an Aries, just know that you've been advised as to how they are and why they're so different from you. I've said previously and will continue to say, any sign can work for you if you have two essential things in your life: God and the right temperament.

CAPRICORN-TAURUS COMPATIBILITY
CHAPTER 22

With this combination, Taurus is actually going to seem more familiar to Capricorn because they are our earth brothers and sisters, as such; many of their traits are very similar to ours. Don't fall into that whole fallacy of "opposites attracting", there is no real truth to that whatsoever. There isn't anything remotely attractive about someone representing everything I do not, or someone who doesn't like to do anything that I like to do, like any of the same foods, like any of the same music, etc. Capricorn and Taurus are faced with the opportunity to have a very happy, harmonious, and comfortable relationship. Both are well rounded, family oriented and take great pride in providing for and protecting their families. They both tend to like nice things, so when you walk into the home of a Capricorn-Taurus couple, more likely than not, that place is going to be fit for a king and queen. Both are very practical and pretty good with money. Taurus can be a little more of a spendthrift than Capricorn, and Capricorn doesn't mind as long as the finances are there and it won't be a strain on the household. These two are very in tuned with each other and depending on their Moon Sign and other surrounding elements, this could be a proverbial "match made in heaven". Taurus is somewhat infamous for their stubborn natures and bad tempers. With the latter though, Taurus has to be pushed to the whole temper thing, like threatening them or their family with harm, totally disrespecting them or their home, no, not happening with Taurus, and Capricorn supports that 100%. They don't "wake up like that" meaning, the temper thing with Taurus has to be brought out. The stubborn nature of both Capricorn and Taurus could cause for a few disagreements here and there, but nothing major, and nothing two earth signs can't get past. They both have a lot in common and are both "sold out" to the relationship once committed. I've heard Capricorns say how they've had awful relationships with Taurus, and how they'll never date a Taurus, and all that, but your tangent toward Taurus is misguided and unfair, because I guarantee you with almost 100% certainty and accuracy, that whatever traits those particular Taurus possessed, that clashed with you, and were not favorable in your relationship with them, more likely than not belonged to whatever their Moon Sign was. Generally speaking Capricorn and Taurus have way too much in common for the relationship not to be balanced and harmonious. Check their Moon Signs, even in retrospect, it could give you some clarity and understanding, then you can stop writing off whole signs based on the actions of a few.

CAPRICORN-GEMINI COMPATIBILITY
CHAPTER 23

This is without question a difficult and extremely challenging match for Capricorn. Truthfully, Capricorns and all air signs are going to be challenging; for several reasons, but the main reason can be pointed to the fact that Capricorns absolutely have to have and thrive on stability, effective communication, continuity, order and discipline. Of the aforementioned, we tend to clash with air signs in pretty much all of those areas; drives us nuts. Put it like this, air signs are infamous for having a lot of "blonde moments" I even voted Aquarius most likely to get lost; but let's deal with Gemini right now. What would be the attraction between the two, aside from an obvious physical attraction. Actually, Gemini's love to learn new things and almost nothing brings them greater joy than to talk or express themselves. Geminis love to talk. For the most part they're fun to talk to, because like Capricorn, a lot of things tend to interest and/or peak their curiosity; they've done a lot of reading and pretty much have a working knowledge about a little bit of everything. Capricorn likes and respects intellect, or someone who speaks with substance and not a bunch of idle chatter and wasted words. Stability is an absolute necessity in the lives of Capricorn. You can't be this way one day, that way the next and other days we don't know what the hell you're going to be on. Unfortunately, Gemini falls into this category. They are also considered "flighty" as well, because they will literally just fall of the face of the earth out the blue for no reason, then reappear like nothing ever happened. This match is chock full of frustration. Capricorn needs to be able to depend on their mate, solid and steady, not indecisive and all over the place.

The way we process information at times is at complete odds and mentally it feels as though we're two ships passing in the night. Capricorn's more reserved and structured nature is in direct contrast with Gemini and their go as it comes, all over the place nature is in direct contrast with Capricorn. This combination would take a lot of patience and adjustments. Capricorns are fully aware that nothing or no-one is perfect, but at some point you have to seriously ask yourselves, does all the constant adjusting, and taking headache medicine, really just equate to the two of you not being compatible for each other, and it may just be better to cut your losses, while at the same time saving what sanity you have left? See, Gemini does love to talk, but when it comes time to walk the walk, Capricorn is all about action; Gemini not so much. I'm not going to beat this in the ground. This is a very challenging combination and you would need an awful lot of patience for this relationship to develop, plus the right temperament to make it last long term.

CAPRICORN-CANCER COMPATIBILITY
CHAPTER 24

Capricorn and Cancer are opposites in the zodiac. It doesn't get any more contrary than that. While in a stripped down, real generic sense, that would seem to indicate that this match is a no-go from the start, and pending doom surely awaits you right? Wrong! Now, I know a lot of Capricorns swear off Cancers and say they're too emotional, they're cry-babies, they're "clingy" they're too sensitive, etc...and all of that maybe true, But upon closer inspection, Capricorn and Cancer have more in common than what meets the eye. I maybe a little more biased because my Moon Sign is in Cancer, so not only do I have a better understanding of who they are and why, I actually possess some of their traits; so quite naturally, I have always been attracted to Cancer and them attracted to me. Capricorn-Cancer, just like Capricorn-Capricorn could be complete hit or complete miss though. I believe with everything in me, that with the right Moon Sign and other astrological elements, Capricorn-Cancer could be that proverbial "match made in heaven". Let me address the pros and cons of this match and why it can be hit or miss, no middle ground. Both Capricorn and Cancer once committed, are dialed in and extremely loyal. Loyalty is everything to Capricorn and they can really appreciate lying down at night knowing that their Cancer is totally devoted to them and the relationship. Both are very in tuned with the other, enjoy and can appreciate quality time together or as a family. Capricorn is normally introverted and Cancers, especially considering what their Moon Sign is, are more extroverted and seems to constantly be on the go; Now this isn't normally a major problem with Capricorn because Cancer at least, will try to include them on their many outings, social gatherings of family and friends, etc... even if Capricorn declines a lot of them because they'd much rather be doing something constructive at home, finishing up some paperwork, a project they were working on, research some things, finish writing on their book, whatever. Now here's where the clashing comes in at. I've addressed it pretty comprehensively that, without an emotionally expressive Moon Sign, most Capricorns are not going to be forthcoming with what and how they feel, Cancer is obviously the opposite, being very expressive and open with their feelings and this could sometimes make Cancer feel as though their Capricorn is cold and doesn't care, which isn't the case, but this trait in Capricorn could cause a clash with Cancer. Yes, Cancers can be "clingy" emotionally and sometimes even physically to an extent, they are normally very emotional and are known to express hurt, joy, pain, whatever through tears. I personally have no problem with anyone displaying feelings or compassion and a heart for something or someone. There's nothing wrong or "weak" about crying or showing emotions, to me, it shows that you're human. I'll take a so-called emotional woman over one who is cold hearted and detached any day of the week. This is a major issue with a lot of Capricorns, especially the ones who are uncomfortable showing or dealing with emotions.

Cancers can also come off as very "needy" as well, this can pose a problem with Capricorn (even me and my moon is in Cancer) because if not careful, neediness can turn into possessiveness in the blink of an eye; and now, "Houston, we have a problem"...With Capricorns, you have to have something going on for yourself that doesn't include them, rather it's a hobby, you belong to a book club, I mean you have to have something that is exclusive to you and not depend totally and completely on your Capricorn mate to be your sole source of fun, or outside social activities. With us, even in relationships, marriage or not, we have to have the freedom and understanding of a significant other, to be able to do our own thing (s) separate from you. This is why the whole clingy/needy thing does not work for Capricorn. It's too restrictive, (Caps do not like feeling restricted) having that kind of responsibility is truthfully unfair for one person, and it can be mentally and emotionally exhausting. I've actually seen and experienced the flip side of this too though. I dated a Cancer (Her Moon Sign is Leo) and she was over the top involved with every facet of what was going on with her family, i.e. mom, dad, sister, grand-dad, everybody. Anytime something happened or needed to get done, they would call her and she would go running over there, I mean, I've never seen someone that controlled by their family. I'm nowhere near "clingy" or needy either, and I casually told her, after observing this behavior for quite some time and never having said a word to her about it; I said, it appears you are essentially married to your family. They pretty much control you and your life. You are at their beck and call and clearly you are ok with this, but no-one should ever be ok with feeling secondary to their significant other's family. As such, this isn't a relationship I feel comfortable moving forward in because for 1. I'm not secondary to anyone and 2. I want a woman that's going to be dedicated to me and our immediate family first and foremost, and apparently your other family takes precedent over your relationship, so, because of that, at this point the relationship you and I had is over and I wish you the best moving forward. I never saw or spoke to her again. Capricorn and Cancer is interesting. I've heard all the murmuring and complaints out there on them, but I'm telling you all right now, with the right elements, Capricorn-Cancer can be an ideal relationship.

CAPRICORN-LEO COMPATIBILITY
CHAPTER 25

As I have mentioned before, a relationship with Capricorn and all of the fire signs are going to be challenging. The same goes for this combination, but the dichotomy is a little different with Capricorn and Leo because we actually have similar traits that both find equally attractive. Both have traits and qualities of strong leaders. Both are normally very conscious and cognizant on a social level. Case in point: President Obama is a Leo and Michelle is a Capricorn (both their Moon Signs are air signs, which would explain their detached, coolness and aloofness. Barack's Moon Sign is Gemini and Michelle's Moon Sign is Aquarius) clearly, they represent intelligence and make a good, strong, capable, power couple right? That's what Capricorn-Leo has the potential to represent, However, Michelle has also went on record as saying, there were plenty of times throughout their marriage, she thought of leaving Barack. That statement speaks directly to the difficulty of Capricorn-Leo. Their approach to just about everything is exactly opposite. Leos are definitely extroverted, social and loves to be out and about. Male Leos are infamous for having a little infidelity problem. Now, this isn't to say all Leos are unfaithful, But their symbol is the Lion for a reason, Lions are known to do what? Hunt right? That's exactly what a lot of Leo men do, they hunt, nuff said. Capricorn doesn't mind being sociable occasionally but they hate being asked or drug to every single social outing by Leo. That speaks to their extroverted nature, and is in direct contrast with introverted Capricorn. They both like nice things, but when it comes to money matters, Capricorn may want to take control of the finances; they tend to be a lot more disciplined in that area than Leo. Just like with Aries, Leo is dominant and tends to be very territorial. I did say that

Capricorn tend to have more spark in the bedroom with the fire signs, but of the 3 Capricorn is least compatible with Leo. Capricorn's conservative nature simply doesn't fit the freaky Leo, and because of our contrast and approach to just about everything, a lot of arguments and quiet moments will likely ensue. Leos make great dads and moms, and are normally very protective of their children, some are even somewhat nurturing, which in itself is kind of odd because of their fiery and dominant natures. If you go out somewhere and see a bunch of guys, yet there's one who is actually the loudest and most boisterous? I'll put my money on him being a Leo. That's how a lot of them are, they need to be in the middle of the happenings, and once there, they have to let their presence be known and they have to be heard. Capricorn is the exact opposite of that and actually find people who are that way, very annoying. Don't go into this one "eyes wide shut". Potential for this relationship to work is there, but it will take a lot of adjustments and compromise. Anybody besides me ever notices Michelle Obama; in all of her pics, always appear to be annoyed or angry? Things that make you go Hmmm...

CAPRICORN-VIRGO COMPATIBILITY
CHAPTER 26

I remember when I first started learning about zodiac signs, and who was and who wasn't compatible with Capricorn. Almost every resource I researched, all unanimously and emphatically stated that Capricorn and Virgo were virtual soul mates, and how this was a "match made in heaven". It further went on to say, that if I found a Virgo, I might as well start making the wedding arrangements, and so on and so forth. Needless to say, I was pretty stoked, thinking, "Wow, a Virgo woman and I would be soul mates huh?" Everyone almost unanimously stated that this relationship was the end all be all for Capricorn. So, I started meeting and dating Virgo women, then the reality eventually settled in. I'm sorry to announce, but those resources and website outlets got it completely wrong. On paper, yes, Virgos are earth signs just like Capricorns, so they will have some very familiar traits, but Virgos have a lot of other traits that greatly annoy Capricorn as well and are not compatible. Virgos, like Capricorns are very dependable, level headed, and are not known to "bust crack head moves"; if our compatibility were based simply on those few things, yes, Capricorn and Virgo would live a lifetime of bliss together; however, we all know, much more is involved in what makes relationships work and what doesn't. A Virgo is not going to be really emotional or affectionate; they tend to show their love by doing something prudent or practical for their significant other. This trait works well for the majority of Capricorns because this is exactly how the majority of us are. Virgos aren't really known to be extremely ambitious, they more so will get a great job or career and stay there; again, this trait works well with Capricorn who is normally very ambitious and there would be no competition between the two because they're both pursuing separate goals and whatnot. In that regard, Virgo would be the perfect complement to Capricorn, is what I'm ultimately saying. Virgos are very unassuming and peaceful, not high strung or abrasive like fire signs, and this works for peaceful Capricorn as well. Now, here is where the clash with Capricorn and Virgo come in at; Virgo women tend to have this "holier than thou" type of attitude and are very motherly; always offering unsolicited advice on what you need to do, how, when, etc...This by itself is extremely nerve wrecking and rubs people the wrong way. They have this sort of fake wholesomeness about themselves like they're so much better than everyone and Capricorn does not get down with that at all. Case in point, this Virgo female was on my Facebook friend's list, I stopped following her because her posts reeked of fakeness and corniness and it was annoying. One day, I guess she wanted to appear really "wholesome" to her little Facebook minions that stroke her virtual and very real ego on the daily via her Facebook Timeline; so she goes on to say how she finally went out on a date after having not been on one in quite some time (hmmm, I wonder why?) and then she says that once she told the guy she wouldn't be having sex with him or anyone unless they were married, the guy thought about and sent her a text saying that he didn't believe, he could, in all honesty go without sex in a relationship, etc...etc.. Ok, cool on both their parts, But what made me say I had had enough of her corniness and unfriended her is when she actually posted the guy's text message on her wall on Facebook for all to see, and of course, on cue, everyone starts praising her for "doing the right thing", and giving her all of this over inflated praise, I had enough of her cornball personality. To me, that was such a huge, unnecessary violation, totally uncalled for; but in her mind, it wasn't about that, it was about what made her look a certain way. Now, don't anyone misconstrue where I'm coming from. I have absolutely no problem with her sticking to whatever her religious morals and values are, the corny part was trying to place them on her sleeve, as some sort of badge or proof that 'she's not like other women', and posting the guy's private and personal text message that was only meant for her to see, is what I felt was 'cornballish' and over the top, but at the same time speaks to this "holier than thou" perception that many Virgos want people to have of them. That's what irked me and pushed me over the edge with her. It was corny, bottom line.

The biggest, and I mean the absolute biggest knock against Virgos are their extreme selfishness. Everything is about them or what works for them, damn if it works for you. They are without a doubt the most self-absorbed individuals of the entire zodiac. Capricorns typically strive to be selfless; Virgos selfishness is in direct contrast with our selflessness. We tend to think of our families first and then us. Virgos tend to think of themselves first, then everyone else, if at all. They are really conscious about their health and yours too if you have any desire to be with them (smokers need not apply). You will rarely find a Virgo, male or female who smokes. They are also very nitpicky and fault finding, quick to point things out about you, yet refuse to take any responsibility or accountability for their personality flaws and shortcomings. That's just it though, to them, they never see themselves as having done anything wrong. The last couple things I just wrote sends Capricorn into another stratosphere of anger and annoyance. We absolutely cannot stand people who refuse to take responsibility for themselves and use that energy to try and become a better person vice using it to make excuses and point at others. On paper, Capricorn-Virgo may appear like that proverbial "match made in heaven", but upon further review, this author has determined that not to be the case. In keeping with my recurring theme of having the proper surrounding elements, Capricorn-Virgo could work, but even with an addition of other traits and qualities, the main ones that does not work for Capricorn will still be there. They're not as bad as this segment suggests, it's just that as a Capricorn, what I'm saying is to not put on the rose-colored glasses and get caught up into how "perfect" this combination could be. It definitely poses some challenges.

CAPRICORN-LIBRA COMPATIBILITY
CHAPTER 27

Capricorn and Libra, generally speaking, is simply a no-go. The biggest frustration for Capricorn with Libra is the communication gap. Libra just does not understand Capricorn, and Capricorn thinks so much differently than Libra. One of Capricorn's biggest pet peeves is repeating themselves; with Libra they seem to have to do that a lot, and it frustrates them to no end. Libra, like all other air signs is detached emotionally, and to a lot of things come off very indifferently. Capricorn may not feel Libra understands or supports their aspirations or endeavors, while Libra just doesn't see what the big deal is. Normally when you first meet someone, aside from the physical attraction, you usually try to build on having some of the same likes, interests, etc...Finding common ground between these two is a task within itself. I don't care how physically attractive you think someone is, to maintain a healthy, harmonious and balanced relationship, there has to be something of substance that acts as the glue that will hold this union together. One thing these two tend to have in common is a talent and love of music. Another thing about music too, is that it can literally bring people together who have totally different backgrounds, ethnicities and cultures. From that perspective, music is pretty powerful. It most certainly has always been a huge staple in my life as I have been blessed with the gift and talent of writing and producing great music ever since I was a small child, and would spend hours doing so in my room alone. Even with this commonality, if Capricorn is expecting Libra to be very engaged, encouraging or even complimentary about their creation of music, think again, Libra, for reasons unknown are simply not very complimentary and are not real big on letting you know how they feel about stuff; so if Capricorn is this way and so are Libra, how is a relationship supposed to flourish if neither is communicating their feelings to one another? And therein lies the basic rift of why a relationship between these two is highly unlikely. Truthfully, it's always going to be a challenge when one of you is an extrovert and one is an introvert. Libras are definitely extroverts with relatively short attention spans, and Capricorn doesn't mind occasionally accompanying you on your social endeavors, but to make this a habitual thing is simply not going to happen. Capricorn has their own goals, interests and agenda, and it normally does not involve going out just for the sake of going out all the time. Now, in the bedroom, Libra and Capricorn make an extremely good match. Libra aims to please and so does Capricorn. The sparks they create in the bedroom, if not careful could probably start a fire. Capricorn takes great pride in their sexual stamina and places a lot of emphasis on performance. Yes, great sex matters to us and from our perspective, you will not get the opportunity to ever say to or about us, that the sex was whack.

CAPRICORN-SCORPIO COMPATIBILITY
CHAPTER 28

This is an interesting combination that actually has great promise and potential. There are a few potential obstacles, as with all relationships really, But let's deal with it. Scorpio, as I've stated previously, could have very easily been a fire sign because of their hair trigger temper. Scorpio, especially when they feel hurt or betrayed can make for a formidable enemy; since revenge is definitely a part of their astrological makeup, I would highly suggest not crossing them the wrong way unless you're prepared to go all the way with it. When and if Scorpio commits to you, trust me, they are ride or die for you, literally. They take their commitments seriously, are very loyal, possessive and tend to be jealous by nature. If you are not ready to commit to Scorpio, don't play games with them. With them, say what you mean and mean what you say. I actually admire their loyalty and serious approach to things, they are not about games, and neither is Capricorn. We share a lot of traits and qualities with Scorpio and why a successful relationship between the two could definitely "be in the cards". Here is where Capricorn and Scorpio could run into problems. Capricorn is all for loyalty and commitment, but we do not possess anyone nor do we want to be possessed. We are of the mindset, that objects are possessed, not human beings. You're supposed to do what you do for your significant other out of a mutual love and respect, not out of obligation. I don't care what your title is, slavery was abolished, no-one "owns' anyone, and sometimes Scorpio's tendency to possess can cause problems in a relationship with Capricorn if not careful. See, here's the thing. With possessiveness, insecurity normally isn't far behind, and right behind that jealousy lurks. I will just state the obvious; none of those aforementioned traits are ingredients for a productive relationship with anyone, not just Capricorn. One thing Capricorn will never lack with Scorpio is support. Much like Capricorn, they are very hands on with their relationships, making sure everything is supposed to be what it is, no stone left unturned if you will. They are totally sold out in their relationships once committed. I guess this would partly explain why they sort of "cling" the way they do. Yes, Scorpios like Cancer (both water signs by the way) have clinging ability, but Scorpio's clinging can be stinging too! Scorpio's tongue, especially when hurt, is right up there with Sagittarius. When hurt, they really don't care, they'll say whatever they have to say to hurt you. Along with their temper, they are also known for their scathing tongues. Sex between Capricorn and Scorpio is off the charts (pun intended). Yes, the chemistry is just that good between these two. Like I said earlier, if Scorpio can keep a tight lid on that little possessiveness thing, Capricorn-Scorpio has potential to be that proverbial "match made in heaven".

CAPRICORN-SAGITTARIUS COMPATIBILITY
CHAPTER 29

Without question, this combination is the consummate oil and water mix. Sagittarius is Capricorn's arch nemesis, I mean, even more so than Aries. Short term, and many of them are extremely short, the few things they both find interesting or even intriguing is not enough to make up for all the extreme differences in temperament, approach, etc... Everything with Capricorn is about order, discipline, sequential even, Sagittarius is more like, whatever, forget all of that let's just do it, kind of reckless in their approach and the way they view and approach things. Sagittarius without question are extroverts who love to travel and truly enjoy learning new things (this is actually a trait them and Capricorn have in common). The absolute biggest knock against Sagittarius is their mouth. They don't believe in filters. They will say whatever comes to their mind regardless of how it comes out and rather or no it offends you, hurts your feelings, etc.... Their lack of tact, horrible timing and unattractive disposition infuriates Capricorn to no end. Sagittarius will never understand Capricorn's "uptightness" and Capricorn will never understand Sagittarius frivolousness and reckless approach to life in general. I actually contemplated writing a book about Sagittarius some years ago, and the title was going to be, "Sagittarius' Are Evil"! You either hate or love them, there is no middle ground with Sagittarius. They tend not to keep friends for any great length of time, because the expectation is that they will eventually say or do something to estrange themselves. Why they are this way is anybody's guess (even mine to an extent) But I find them intriguing which is why I was going to write a book on them. Many of them, are fixated on the devil or the "dark side" of things, I've always found that really interesting, which made me want to research them on a much deeper level. That said, I started with their symbol, which many of you know is a CENTAUR , or a half man/half horse. Ok, that symbol by itself is an unholy one, because it represents bestiality. Hmmm, ok, now I'm even more intrigued right? So the questions still lingered in my mind, why is Sagittarius so hated, why are many of them fixated on Satan and the dark side, why are they like, expected to do or say something foul, and not even care how it makes someone feel? Why are Sagittarius considered the untamable of the Zodiac, and what the hell is up with this centaur? Well, let's see if some information on what centaurs were can shed some light on why Sagittarius' are the way they are and do some of the things that they do:

"The centaur is a mythological creature. Its head, arms, and chest are those of a human and the rest of its body, including four legs, hindquarters, and a tail is like that of a horse. Centaurs lived in herds on Mt. Pelion in Thessaly, Greece, and were a plague to the people around them. They went about drunk, eating raw flesh, trampling crops, and raping female humans. The intellectual parts they inherited from humankind left them ignorant and yet cunning.

The Centaurs were creatures that were sometimes very hostile towards humans. They were always involved in brawls and battles. Often Zeus would send the Centaurs to punish gods and humans who had offended him. The hostility between man and Centaurs is said to have originated when the Centaurs were invited to their stepbrother's (Pirithous), wedding celebration. At the feast Eurytion, one of the Centaurs, becoming intoxicated with the wine, attempted to offer violence to the bride; the other Centaurs followed his example, and a dreadful conflict arose in which several of them were slain.

The wicked centaurs are the antithesis of the knight and the horseman. Instead of mastering or taming their instincts, these centaurs are ruled by them. They symbolize violent lust, adultery, brutality, vengefulness, heretics, and the Devil. They represent the struggle within each heart between good and evil, moderation and excess, passion and propriety, forgiveness and retaliation, belief and unbelief, god and beast." (Centaurs, 2009)

So there it is there. Majority of my questions were answered. And see ladies and gentleman, what I just read lends credence to my position that we are Universally aligned with the symbols that represent us astrologically in some form or fashion. The symbols of the Zodiac are not random, or by chance. They are very deliberate, meaningful and if studied closer and correctly can and will reveal a lot about who you are. It's kind of ironic that they used the word antithesis to describe centaurs, because that is exactly how I view Sagittarius in relation to Capricorn, they are without question, our antithesis. What I love about them though, is that with Sagittarius, they're not going to be fake, they like you or they don't. They are truly no frills, you never have to wonder where they're coming from because they have no problem telling you where they're coming from and why. They are extremely honest, sometimes brutally, Capricorns can relate to that because we can be brutally honest as well; the difference is, we use tact and understand the importance of the art of timing. My grandmother always said, it's not what you say, but how you say it. Sagittarius clearly does not live by that mantra or subscribe to its principle. Sex between Capricorn and Sagittarius is off the charts; of all the fire signs, they are the most compatible with Capricorn. I personally have had some of my best sex with Sagittarius. I dated one, and it was so good, even though we broke up, she literally asked if we could still have sex occasionally. So, yeah, no problems in that area between these two. Too bad you can't live a relationship totally in the bedroom, because if that was the case, Capricorn and Sagittarius could coexist and live happily ever after for real. No, after all the "oooos and ahhhhs", you both have to get up and either co-exist or co-habitate. No level of great sex will ever be able to totally sustain a relationship; it may be able to prolong the inevitable, but sustain? No, at least not long term. Approach this one, as all relationships really, with an open mind (you never know), but with realistic expectations.

CAPRICORN-CAPRICORN COMPATIBILITY
CHAPTER 30

I have read all the complaints, grumblings and murmurings, about two Capricorns being too much alike for a relationship to work, and yada, yada, yada. First off, that whole being too much alike business has been regurgitated by everyone and their mama for as long as I can remember, and again, there is no truth to this long held "belief", it's truly a fallacy. I have never in my life met or interviewed anyone who broke up because they were "too much alike"; you normally break up with someone because of your differences, especially in the areas that really matter to you. I personally have never broken up with any female because we were "too much alike". I wish I could find a woman more like me, especially in the considerate and caring department, I'd set the wedding date! Now, with that said, let me say for the record, Two Capricorns in a love match is the most ideal in the Zodiac. Capricorn-Capricorn can literally be 100% hit or 100% miss though. The challenge is finding one, who has a comparable Moon Sign that will be compatible with yours, otherwise, two Capricorns could be "clash" and not like each other very much at all. This is mostly because of the Moon Sign; there are other elements as I've stated earlier, within your Astrological Chart that play a part in compatibility as well, but your Moon Signs being compatible, I'd say, takes precedence over the other elements in your chart. For example, My Sun/Moon Combo is Capricorn/Cancer (which means I have the personality traits of both signs), if I met a female whose Sun/Moon combo was Capricorn/Aquarius...9 times out of 10 we're going to clash, not because we're both Capricorns, No! Because My Moon Sign of Cancer is not compatible with her Moon Sign of Aquarius (Emotionally our approach in relationships are complete opposites!) In Astrology, compatibility truthfully lies in the Moon Signs of each individual, more so than the Sun signs. This is why I've been stressing for you all to know yours and your mates Moon Sign, because you and them carry the traits of whatever it is as well as your birthday sign (sun sign). Here's a small list of reasons, why a relationship with two Capricorns would work and why it wouldn't.

Why it would work:

1. Both have the same values and ideals about family
2. Both are hard workers and goal oriented
3. Both are conservative but appreciate nice things
4. Both are loyal and committed to the relationship once dialed in
5. Both understand the "bigger picture" where goals are concerned
6. Both understand and appreciate ambition
7. Both will support each other's drive
8. Both tend to be visionaries
9. Both are dependable
10. They both have a measure of the spirit of wisdom

Why they would Clash:

1. Having incompatible Moon Signs
2. Both wanting to play the same role
3. Nonspecific definition of roles in the relationship
4. One not operating in the spirit of compromise (cause both can be very stubborn, with 2 Caps, it has to be give and take)

Here's a comprehensive breakdown of 2 Capricorns in a love match:

"Similar goals and similar needs in love provide a healthy and solid foundation for the partnership of Capricorn man and woman. No matter how different they are on other levels, the

fact that their relationship needs are comparable can help smooth out their pairing. Each of them can be a little shy or standoffish at first when it comes to getting to know each other intimately.

Capricorn man's determination is followed by outstanding patience. He is very ambitious and has a strong head to fulfill all his dreams. He appears to want to be alone but longs for admiration and acceptance from people just like everyone else. He is very stable and does not appreciate changes at all. In a relationship, he is a truly committed lover with strong qualities of caring and protecting his lady love.

A Capricorn woman is an ultimate lady with all the feminine characteristics together with a practical mind and a truly caring heart for her loved ones. It is very difficult to define the characteristics profile of a Capricorn girl exactly. She can be the sexy babe on the beach or a scientist sitting in the laboratory, doing experiments that can save mankind. Whatever she is on the outside, when looked inside, there is a girl who needs security, authority, respect and position. It is an entirely different matter how she seeks to achieve these goals.

They both are very conventional in their ways of thinking. They spend a lot of time making sure that their significant other is liked and loved by their family. She usually fulfills all the criterions for being a perfect match for a Capricorn man as she is also smart and family oriented just like him. She makes a perfect wife and takes proper care of his family, her family and definitely the family they both make together. She is gentle; she is kind and admires his ambitious nature and strong determination but she can be bossy sometimes.

Both the Capricorn man and Capricorn woman is very ambitious and he always respects this about her. These two hold great admiration for each other. They are very much alike holding the same morals and values, therefore it is very easy for them to understand each other. Together, they provide a great support system for each other. He is very structured and follows a routine which gives a sense of stability to her. He always cares and protects his Capricorn lady and takes her word seriously. He helps her to see eye-to-eye on how you spend and save money. Both of them are able to save for a rainy day and hence enjoy financial security in their relationship. But sometimes he may show some domination which is usually not entertained by Capricorn woman and this can cause minor issues between them

The Capricorn man and woman make one of the most compatible relationships with many things in common and yet just enough differences to keep the relationship stimulated. Their love has stability and their oneness is peaceful. They both are sensual beings and understand each other's needs quite well. As the love between them increases, they understand the importance of love and become more expressive towards each other. As the mountains are blessed with mighty view, their love is blessed with calmness that is experienced by very few. They enjoy silver winters with warmth of their love, blossomy spring with colors of their devotion and summers with the breezy understanding. Nothing can ever ruin the relationship which is as firm as that of Capricorn man and woman, once they decide to be together with the most prosperous family life.

As both Capricorn man and woman are earthy in nature, they possess a sensuality that is impossible to escape. Both are low at verbal expression but unfailingly express their love through their sexual oneness. They are able to release all of those emotions they keep buried throughout the day during love making. Seeing how the lovemaking between the two of them is a release, it can become quite explosive. These two fit like a glove in the bedroom. One could compare their love making to that of the excitement of the invention of a new romance. Each and every time is a new discovery. There is nothing better than making love to someone who can be trusted and understands the needs of the other and both the Capricorns are compatible enough to give what the other requires. The lovemaking is a very passionate and dynamic act for both, the Capricorn woman and Capricorn man. Their lovemaking is a cleansing process that rids their bodies of tainted emotions and stress and brings them closer, making them one in all aspects of life.

Capricorn man and woman both love their own families dearly and are extremely protective of the family they create together. Each one of them is vulnerable in some sense. If each of them is so well put together, then each of them feels as though their protective nature is being wasted. One needs to be stronger, where the other is weak. In order for the Capricorn woman and Capricorn man to love one another they have to find those vulnerabilities in one another, and then they will feel needed. Feeling needed creates a true love between two people. As long as they can learn to open up to each other, they find a life time of love. They also find a deep love in the family they create together." (Ask Oracle, 2015)

CAPRICORN-AQUARIUS COMPATIBILITY
CHAPTER 31

This is a challenging combination. Just like their other air sign predecessors, the communication and comprehension gap between these two probably provides the widest margin in a potential relationship being successful. Aquarius' are "go getters"... Capricorn is attracted to that in them. They have a penchant for "getting to the money" and they are pretty good with money management, mostly because, for all their love of "getting money" they are infamous for being "cheap"; I mean, Aquarian women look for the bargain in every single thing, it doesn't matter if they have a dollar or a thousand dollars in their pockets, they refuse to and will not pay full price for anything. Many of them have this trait really bad too, and they honestly can't help it. That's just how they are. Capricorns are far from being wasteful with money, but this trait in Aquarius can and would drive us nuts. Actually the qualities and traits Capricorn and Aquarius are normally attracted to in each other is probably better suited for a business partnership/relationship, because a romantic pairing of these two leaves too much to be desired, and way too many adjustments to be worth all the extra headache and antacid that would have to be involved to make it work. Temperament is definitely the key. I'm pretty sure there are some Capricorns out there who have the patience and temperament to be in a romantic relationship with an Aquarius, I'm just not one of them. They are loyal though and fun to talk to because they love learning new and exciting things. Capricorn lives, breathes and thrives on effective communication. Sometimes we can explain something to

Aquarius every which way to Sunday and they still don't and won't get it, and words can't express how extremely frustrating this is for Capricorn. Aquarius are normally very detached emotionally and are not going to be the affectionate, "lovey-dovey" types at all, so if you are one of those Capricorns that require and desire affection (privately and publicly) Aquarius is definitely not going to work for you. To their credit, Aquarius will give you all they're capable of giving, and at the end of the day, you really can't be mad at that. My thing is this, people are who they are, irrespective of astrological sign. You can and are willing to deal with them or you can't and you don't. It's really as simple as that. I never met a single woman I wanted to try and change. No, you be you, and let me see if I'm equipped or willing to deal with what and whoever you are, and vice versa, I mean, fair enough right? On the surface, there is definitely some challenges with this combination, but with the right elements, it actually has potential to be successful, or at the very least sustainable.

CAPRICORN-PISCES COMPATIBILITY
CHAPTER 32

In a potential relationship, of the water signs, Pisces is probably an even tougher sell than Cancer in many cases. It's not that the potential or the temperament isn't there because it is; it's other intangibles at play that could doom this union. First off, Pisces tend to be "sweet" and very non-discriminate (depending on their Moon Sign too though!) They are very quiet, likable and pretty much get along with everyone. They don't want any drama with anyone (again, this also depends on what their moon is) Pisces women tend to be really prissy and "girly-girly", I'm talking their hair, nails, the way they dress, everything. Normally, they tend to be ultra-feminine. Hey, that works for me. I love a woman who takes pride in her appearance and is in close touch with her femininity, sensuality and sexuality. Many of them are like peace makers and it's truthfully difficult to even get angry with a lot of Pisces. Their personalities and aura is that of peace and very non-threatening. Quiet as it's kept, Christ was actually born under the sign of Pisces (he's a symbolic Capricorn, He was not actually born December 25th, surprisingly, this will come as a shock to many of you) and many traits they possess are some of the exact same ones he possessed. A lot of Pisces also tend to view themselves as martyrs (Martin Luther King Jr's Moon Sign was Pisces, martyr indeed, see, it lines up doesn't it, because Christ was the ultimate martyr) Now, with everything I just said, you're probably thinking, they sound like the "perfect mate" right? But here's where the problem with Pisces comes in at. A lot of Pisces have a penchant for not telling the whole truth and not being very forthcoming with information about themselves. They are very secretive, and make getting to know them, especially in the beginning, like pulling teeth. Truthfully it doesn't matter how long you've been with a Pisces, they're not going to ever just like, tell you everything. That's just their nature. If you press too much on them, especially in the beginning stages of "getting to know them" They'll simply pull a Gemini on you and just disappear. No text, no phone, call, no speech, nada, just *poof* they're 'outta' there! So, it's not their temperament or anything along those lines because all of that fits Capricorn perfectly, plus the fact that they, like Capricorn need their "replenish time" or time to themselves, so again, we line up there; but at the end of the day, their secretive nature speaks more to rather or not we would be able to trust them. That's the deal breaker right there. When Capricorn lies down at night, next to their significant other, they want to know and feel through and through, that the person lying next to them has their side, front and back and there are no worries or concerns over their truthfulness. With them it's a potential trust issue.

MOST-LEAST DESIRABLE TRAITS OF ALL 12 SIGNS
CHAPTER 33

Truthfully, we all have our "good and bad" qualities, doesn't matter what your sign is. That said, here's a list of the most and least desirable traits of all 12 signs of the Zodiac:

Aries
Most Desirable- fearless, relentless (never say die) adventurous
Least Desirable- Volatile, impatient, bullies (loves to pick fights)

Taurus
Most Desirable- committed, protectors, dependable
Least Desirable- stubborn, can develop one track mind, temper

Gemini
Most Desirable- talkative, loves learning new things, open minded
Least Desirable- 'Flippy'/Flighty, inconsistent, detached and dismissive

Cancer
Most Desirable- caring, loving, generous, loyal, ride or die for theirs
Least Desirable- can be ultra-sensitive (wears feelings on sleeves and sometimes feelings are hurt easily), clingy (emotionally and physically)

Leo
Most Desirable-social (knows no stranger, loves to be out and about, protectors, make good parents
Least Desirable- cheaters (most have major problem with fidelity), arrogant, can never seem to stay home

Virgo
Most Desirable- dependable, most are very health conscious, very even tempered
Least Desirable- selfish, very self-absorbed, loves to give unsolicited advice

Libra
Most Desirable- easy to get along with, no frills (it is what it is with them), most have a penchant or talent for music
Least Desirable- indecisive, non-dependable, flighty

Scorpio
Most Desirable- high sexual appetite and energy, loyal, committed
Least Desirable- possessive, jealous, scathing tongue when hurt, vengeful

Sagittarius
Most Desirable- No frills (they like you or they don't) open minded, easy to talk to, loves to travel
Least Desirable- no filter, say what comes to their mind with no regard for how it comes out, mean, does not like to be tied down

Capricorn
Most Desirable- ambitious, protectors, loyal, no-nonsense, family oriented, committed, focused, hard workers, compassionate, generous, dependable, wise, ride and die for theirs
Least Desirable- Can be very dismissive and intolerant,

tend to live our lives behind a wall not many get invited over to, can be very black or white with no leeway or middle in between, you're either with us or against us

Aquarius
Most Desirable- ambitious, very creative in ways of making money, open minded, loves to learn new things
Least Desirable- cheap, looks for the bargain in everything, tend to have a lot of "blonde moments", emotionally detached

Pisces
Most Desirable- friendly, peaceful spirits, easy to talk to, very compassionate and caring about others
Least Desirable- not always fully truthful, very secretive, flighty

KNOWLEDGE, WISDOM AND UNDERSTANDING
CHAPTER 34

"When you know what you're talking about, people tend to want to hear what you have to say"- Anonymous

I have built up a tremendous following for my writings, daily inspirational and educational postings dealing with everything from life, relationships, spiritual understanding, encouragement, enlightenment on various things, philosophy, etc....the wisdom that normally fills these words I take no credit for, But the response to them has been nothing short of tremendous, humbling and encouraging at the same time. I have been blessed with the spirit of knowledge, wisdom and understanding. As such, I'm more than likely going to have to publish a separate book with all of them. For now though, here is a really nice collection of my many words and hopefully you all will get some type of higher level of understanding, consciousness, inspiration, encouragement or enlightenment from them. I give all praise to THE MOST HIGH, it is by Him from whence these words of wisdom flow.

There is no statute of limitation on success

live your life, make mistakes, learn from those mistakes, regret nothing and plan for tomorrow, but live for today
Take inventory of everything that's currently going on in your life and everyone that's in it; what's right, what's wrong, how can it be better, and what can you do to improve your situation. Be brutally honest, look in the mirror, and don't be afraid of the reflection, it's just a representative of you currently, but, you and only you can change that for the

future. If you have a bunch of dead weight in your life, get rid of it because all its doing is holding you down and back from your true destiny. You can lose all of your money, your house, car, etc...but all of that you can get back, time is something once wasted is lost and gone forever; you can't get it back. If you want a better situation and the person or persons currently in your life aren't helping you get there, then they're hurting you.

Jealousy is like a cancer that slowly eats away at your soul

I'm personally at a point in my life, where I am no longer seeking friendships. I seek to form alliances. The word "friend" now-a-days is thrown around loosely with no real sense of responsibility attached to it. Even the term "best friend" or bff, seems to now be inter-changeable. Allies are people that will literally go to war with you, and you never have to worry which side they're on either; somebody come messing with you, they're right there, and vice versa. An alliance is a bond where you both share common goals, interests, ideologies and will do what you have to do to protect them. If Judas was Jesus' ally...We don't have the crucifixion. The introspection here is deep, but something to think about.

Throughout my studies in behavioral science over the years, there's a quality that I rarely if ever talk about, in addition to how the Zodiac affects Human Behavior;(I personally call it "The 5th Element") which to me, is a metaphor for learned behavior. My personal hypothesis as a behaviorist is that, irrespective of what our astrological charts are, a lot of what we do, who and what we become, how we react to things/people, etc...Can be traced back to where we grew up, what our parent (s) taught us, and what our experiences were as children. A lot of behavior is learned, consciously and subconsciously; because as children, we are most vulnerable and most impressionable. Can learned behavior be un-learned? That is the age old question that will continue to be debated probably until the end of time. I liken learned behavior to a form of brain-washing. For years, you were taught a certain thing, so quite naturally, over time, that behavior was accepted by you as "normal" and adopted by virtue of you incorporating it into your everyday life/life-style. If you constantly tell a child, that they're nothing and will never amount to anything, as hard for some to believe what I just typed, but many children are spoken to this way, and by the person who is supposed to mean the most to them as a child or as an adolescent. Well, it shouldn't come as a big shock when the child grows up and has all sorts of behavioral problems, getting into trouble in school (this is how and where it normally starts), making the wrong choices, in and out of jail, etc...You can't continuously set someone up for failure, then wonder why they've failed. That defies logic, reason and common sense.

I truly wish everyone in this world had an open mind, hunger and desire to learn the powers and "mysteries" of this Universe to help them make better decisions and become better human beings. Astrology is one of the great powers of the Universe and if only people would step outside of the regurgitated, brain washed rhetoric, they would be able to see that. God created the zodiac and it is extremely powerful and relevant to every single person ever born into this world with respect to human behavior.

The day a woman loses respect for her man, that's pretty much the beginning of the end of that relationship. Men should never, under any circumstance, relinquish their position as head of their family unless it's in death. Just because a woman is strong enough to hold down a family on her own does not mean she should, nor how God ordained it. Men need to step back into their roles and rightful positions in the home, with a strong woman by your side helping you lead, not carrying the burden or shouldering the whole load.

Men sometimes may go through a phase where they lose their job, are laid off, or whatever the case may be, and they're struggling to get back where they once were, that's when having a strong woman is going to come to mean the most. You hold each other down, for better or for worse. Whatever situation comes up, you tackle it, and do whatever you have to do, to get through it together. Kings need Queens, Presidents need First Ladies, we need one another. The sooner many realize this, instead of explaining away, or fooling yourself into believing you don't, the quicker families can become complete and stronger again, as we raise our little men and women to value the exact same things and continue to pass it on as we break that cycle of fatherlessness, dysfunction and broken families.

There's no such thing as being "independent" in a marriage, as husband and wife you are Interdependent, and that must be your mind set; if not, you need to recondition your mentality, to one that's suitable, productive and conducive to marriage and everything the covenant of marriage is supposed to mean.

Yes, we are all imperfect and not without flaws, categorized by those who will accept that and strive daily to become an overall better person, then there are those who refuse to accept any responsibility for their imperfections, therefore end up in a never ending cycle of bad relationships and un-happiness. If you keep taking the same bad attitude, the same selfishness, the same self-absorption, and the same arrogance into a new relationship, you are destined to keep repeating the same results. I'm so tired of hearing women say, "I'm a work in progress", but back that up with nothing tangible. There are women that have been saying that for over 10 years, at some point you have to say, ok, is that affirmation rhetorical? Accepting that you have flaws is step one in the process of self-improvement. Once you truly accept that, then the 2nd step is to take action (remember faith without works is dead) to change that behavior that's keeping you stagnated in your relationships, your job, etc. You can't successfully endure your journey without the spirit of humility.

We are all subject to Universal Laws, Which dictates that there is a Universal Order to things. What does that mean? It means there is a time and season for all things; There is a time to laugh and a time to cry, a time we all live, a time we all die, there is a time to speak and a time to be silent...Because we have certain manifest powers, many of us miss our season, i.e our blessings, not knowing when to speak and when to be silent. Wisdom, which can only come from THE MOST HIGH, will let you know when to do what. What you don't want to do, is become your own worst enemy because you don't know when to table your tongue.

If you want a different result, you will have to start making a different decision. Sometimes it's what a person doesn't say, that speaks the loudest. You truthfully never even have to ask anyone where you stand in their lives, Their actions will tell you everything you need to know; You don't need any further validation.

A true friend or mate should want you to do better for yourself, and encourage you in that spirit. Some people you just have to "love" from a distance. That's why The Bible says, sometimes 'you have to come out from among them and be ye separated'. It's never too early or too late to evaluate your life, and do some early or late spring cleaning.

There's almost nothing more annoying than someone who refuses to take responsibility and accountability for their wrong doing (s) Instead of humbling themselves and apologizing for having wronged you, or making you feel a certain way, they'd rather add insult to injury and let their pride stroke their ego and over inflated view they already have of themselves.

Be very conscious and aware of who's in your circle. So-called family included, because the Jealous Spirit is one of the oldest in existence, and knows no bounds. As a matter of fact, a jealous spirit can turn into a Judas one real quick. Just because they say they're happy for you doesn't mean they really are, Just because they smile in your face doesn't mean they're your friend, and everyone who says they're "praying for" you could be secretly praying against you, Believe that...Pray for a discerning spirit, to help you with all of the above, that way, you can expose them for their true intention, and not fall for the fake words coming out of their mouth. Christ was sinless and the most perfect human being that ever walked the face of the earth; all he did was heal the sick, make the lame walk, raise the dead, etc...And He is still hated, to this day, and has enemies. Don't think for one second you don't, the key is being able to weed them out.

A man can have the love and adoration of a thousand women, but it only takes one to capture his heart.

Sometimes a man or woman's job is to come into your life to get you ready for the one God truly has for you! Once they've served their reason and their season? Don't try to hold on, Let them go, Trust, They were just a place holder; Nobody God ordains you to be with, would even entertain the thought of leaving. They weren't meant for you, accept that and move on, toward your ultimate destiny.

The spirit of compromise is essential in all successful relationships. What you both feel is equally important, the key and sometimes the challenge is finding common ground between what you both feel, and that can sometimes be extreme in contrast. Hence. compromise. As long as you're committed to coming to an agreeable and comfortable solution, realizing at the end of the day, that it's not about you, but rather about the both of you, then the love and respect you have for each other is the best mediator you could ever hope to have and make any agreement digestible; at the end of the day, all you both really want is for each other to be happy, right?

Sometimes you have to just step out on faith and not be

afraid to fail. Success comes and goes, but true failure comes in the form of not even trying.

You can't expect something from someone that you aren't giving, or 100% willing to give. For every action you take, there is going to be an equal or greater reaction, so if you're constantly getting the same reaction, but from different people? That's confirmation that some adjustments are in order to the person staring back at you in the mirror.

Being a "control freak"

I'll state the obvious and say, This is not an endearing quality, nor will it win you a lot of popularity contests. Normally, there are a couple of other adjectives that like to "hang out" with control freaks; being demanding, having a healthy dose of narcissism, (contrary to what they believe in their heads, it is not all about them) self-serving, authoritarian, dictatorial, inconsiderate, just to name a few. As you can see, control freaks do not keep good company with this personality trait. You ever see or hear of those people in old folks home, who nobody ever comes to visit? I know, sad right? but I guarantee you, if you talk to some of them, and they are open and very honest about the life they've lived, it won't surprise you to uncover that many of them were control freaks who effectively alienated everyone out of their lives, sometimes even their own children. Yeah, it's really that serious. No-one wants to be controlled or made to feel less important than you are. In a relationship, you do what you do for one another out of mutual love and respect. The key word is mutual, i.e. it's not about you, it should be about "us"...Compromise in a relationship is not an option, it's a necessity; especially if you want a healthy and productive one over a long period of time, and hopefully the rest of your life. Sincere self-reflection, if you are honest with yourself, can reveal the need for change, or at the very least, the need to make a personality adjustment. How are you continuing to approach everything and everybody the same exact way, then act confused and bewildered as to why you keep getting the same results? Just so you know, Control freaks are a major turn off, and if they're not careful, they're going to be that old person who no-one ever comes to visit. I thank God for the gift of writing and putting words together well via a sometimes deep and very introspective thought process; and it is my sincere hope that many of you continue to get some type of encouragement, enlightenment or understanding through from my words.

I know many of you are sick and tired of going through failed relationship after failed relationship, can't seem to advance on your job, or get that great paying job you've been seeking, some days you feel like your life is just stuck in a rut basically, *"Treadmillin"* is what I call it, ***running fast as hell, but going nowhere.*** To put all of the aforementioned in perspective, you have to understand that there is a Universal Order to things, In Biblical terms, a time and season for all things...And it's simply just not your season yet, that's all. You have to keep moving forward though, and it's ok to be disappointed, that's a natural human emotion; Don't linger too long on it though because if it consumes you it can render you inactive, take a deep, deep breath, blow it out and continue moving forward. Time waits for no man. When it's your season? You will prosper and succeed in everything you touch, and that phrase "get it while the getting is good" will have a whole new meaning in your life, Hang in there your season is coming, Just don't lose hope, focus or faith, and never under any circumstance give up!

When someone makes you feel a certain way, and you express that to them, and what it was they said or did that contributed to you feeling that way? Truth is, they may never understand why, what they did or said made you feel a certain type of way, because your feelings are yours, and we all respond to certain stimuli differently. Enough with the "I'm just trying to understand..." Well, you may never understand why someone feels what they do, Which is why all you have to do is respect that they feel that way and not repeat the behavior that contributed to it.

Normally people on the outside looking in, are giving you advice from an obstructed view.

Some people who come into our life are simply a rest stop on your journey to somewhere else.
Potential in a man should count for something. He may not be "all that" today, But you have to look at the overall resume and package. If that man is educated, driven, has goals, short and long term with a viable, realistic plan on how to achieve them? Don't be so quick to judge him on what he doesn't have today. Just because you may be "up" now, have a nice job, car, etc...You didn't always have what you have either, and how would you honestly feel if men judged rather or not they should date you on what you didn't have? The right man or woman by your side can help elevate you to much greater heights, but you'll never know that if you fall victim to what I call the *"Now Syndrome"*...There's a huge difference between a man who has goals, dreams and aspirations, But may have fallen on a bad time trying to get back on his feet, than some bum who has no goals, drive or inspiration to do or have anything more than he has today. There was this young man who didn't have a job, a car or a house of his own, but he was fresh out of College with a whole lot of goals and big dreams. He met his future wife while she was working at her job, and he showed up looking for one. Although that young man in the "now" didn't have much, she didn't judge him on that, she saw his potential. and gave him a shot. They are now married with 2 beautiful daughters and He is The President of The United States and she is The First Lady. Don't be so quick to write somebody off, you could be just what's needed to help in that elevation to the next level; but you will never know that if you continue to unfairly judge others on where they are today.

Rejection is difficult to deal with on any level, and one of the most hurtful of all human emotions, But sometimes that's just God's way of saying he has something or someone better for you; So don't think of it as being rejected, think of it simply, as you're just being redirected.

While I don't subscribe to the theory that time "heals" all wounds, What it does do, is help push it further into our sub-conscious, so at least it doesn't affect you mentally, physically or emotionally any longer or as much. Refocus your energy on where God is redirecting you. It's a waste of time and energy to A. worry about a situation you cannot control and B. worry about someone who isn't the least concerned about you. Remember, The most perfect man who walked this earth, was without sin, healed the sick, made the lame walk, and even he was and is rejected by many. When you put your rejection in that context? It pales in comparison and should give you the extra added inspiration and motivation to simply keep moving forward. Life is a blessing as evidenced by our waking, each and every day. The key is to keep moving forward at all costs and do not under any circumstance go back. If God meant for us to go backwards HE would have put our feet on that way.

Ladies: If a Man truly loves you nothing in this world can keep him away from you, but if he doesn't love you anymore and for whatever reason has lost all interest in your relationship, nothing you do or say can make him stay; As hurtful as it may be to accept, you should never try to hold on to someone who obviously doesn't care about losing you. He's actually doing you a favor and you just can't see it yet...What favor is that you might ask if he's leaving you? Him leaving is making room for the Man you're really supposed to be with.

The foundation of a solid and productive relationship is based on trust, open, honest and consistent communication, consideration and respect. And to illustrate the point further, if either one of those is missing, there is going to be a disconnect in that relationship. Sooner, or later, depending on how bad or to what degree the behavior is being exhibited. You can't disrespect someone, then act surprised or play the victim when you are disrespected in return; you have no right to expect anything from anyone that you aren't giving or are willing to give. Whatever you give, be prepared to get right back, That's a Universal Law. So many people have what I call, the *"Great I Syndrome"*, ***The ones who see themselves as never doing anything wrong***, and on top of that refuse to take responsibility or accountability for any of their actions; instead, what do they do? They dismiss all who don't fall in line with their BS or kiss their butts. 10 times out of 10, those are the ones who end up old and alone wondering what happened and how come they don't have anyone; I'll help you out, Look in the mirror, that's the reason you don't have anyone, because everyone wasn't wrong and you were the only one right your entire life; Clearly you needed to make adjustments in your behavior, how you treat people, etc... But instead, you kept the same attitude, same approach, same mind set to every single relationship without trying to change a single thing, and got the same result, "Being a work in progress" is just a tired cliche' and a crutch if the person isn't making any conscious and concerted effort (s) to change or adjust their behavior, mindset and approach for the better. All the money and material comfort in the world will never take the place of having a significant other to share your life with; share your joys, pains, disappointments, laughs, tears, etc.. (that's exactly why there's a whole bunch of lonely and miserable millionaires) So now, what you've done is effectively run everyone out of your life, now it's just you, Old, bitter and alone Just the way you wanted it right? Ladies, Please, Don't let this be you. We are all perfectly imperfect, the key is to acknowledge that and be willing to strive, each day, to be a better person, a better mother, wife, husband, son, daughter, etc... And overall a better human being. Humble yourselves, there's a reason God gives grace to those that do.

You don't need to have a lot of money to add value to someone's life.

Self-worth does not require a cosigner

Ignorance is not confined to a particular race or gender, it's free, doesn't discriminate and you can get it anywhere

In life, Dead weight can hold you back from your destiny just like any other contributing factor, if you allow it. Dead weight are considered people who add no value to your life whatsoever, do not encourage or inspire you in any way. When it's all said and done, they're either part of the problem or part of the solution. If your significant other doesn't inspire, encourage or support your dreams and aspirations, Then I would say that is actually pretty significant, and something to really think about. If someone truly loves you like they proclaim, they would want you to reach your full potential and encourage you to reach for your goals and go for your dreams.

Red flags are red for a reason: It Universally means to stop! When you see and experience red flags in your new relationship? The worst thing you can do is either ignore it or make excuses for it. Things like petty jealousy, being controlling and insecurity does not normally get better with time. You need to stop and seriously reflect on rather or not that's going to be a good situation for you, long or short term.

Life is truly about living, loving, being loved and giving back. THE MOST HIGH blesses us so we can be a blessing to others. I truthfully don't remember all the good I've done for others throughout my life because it was never about that with me, and I've never kept score. Truthfully, I didn't do anything, God did it through me, and everyone who knows me know this is not a fake act of humility on my part; I feel this way with everything inside me. All the praise, honor and thanks is due Him, not me. I am just a willing and able vessel that came along at a time in someone's life, when they were at a low point, and really needed a blessing, no strings attached;

and our Heavenly Father sent me because He trusted me in this capacity. This is who and how He made me to be and why I have always been blessed, even throughout those times in my life when it was hard for me to see it right away. I don't care what I go through, I could and would never think of complaining about anything. God has done too much for me and for those I've loved and cared about to call myself trying to complain about anything. If He never does another single thing for me in this life time, Father, you've done enough.

A couple of the worst feelings of all human emotions is to feel unaccepted or unappreciated. I have always been of the mindset that no-one has to do anything for you, and it doesn't matter what their title is, so when they do something nice or thoughtful, the very least anyone can do is to show appreciation for that; Because although it sounds kind of cliche', it truly is the thought that counts. Being considered or thought of is priceless, the problem is too many people now-a-days, take even the smallest gestures for granted. Then after a while, wonder why there is a disconnect in their relationship. No-one wants to continuously and constantly feel like what they do, doesn't matter. It's disheartening and discouraging.

Happiness is a choice
Sometimes it's best to walk the road less traveled, by taking ownership of your part in a disagreement/argument, Beg the pardon of the person you're having the misunderstanding/disagreement with and keeping it moving. Life is too short to be arguing and bickering over silly stuff and pettiness. It's not about who's right or who's wrong all the time, because truth be told, by nature, no human likes to be wrong, but peace trumps disorder and chaos any day, which is why we should always strive for it.

Just because you've believed something your entire life, doesn't make it the truth; and just because you don't believe something, doesn't mean it's a lie either.

If someone tells you one thing, but does something else,

believe what they do.

I understand fully when you're really passionate about something or even someone, you want to literally shout it at the top of your lungs at every given opportunity. Many feel this way about GOD, and I'm not mad at that at all. HE is my source and His son, The Christ is my Lord and Savior, and I make no apologies for that. However, I will say this, your love and passion for GOD should help lead others to him not turn them off and away. Some people you can't even have a "regular" conversation with them, because they're so "holy rolly" everything out their mouth is God this God that, and honestly for those who aren't anywhere near where you profess to be in Him, that can not only be intimidating, but somewhat frustrating and disheartening even. Reason being, you appear unreachable, and to someone who genuinely cares about you this can be really disappointing. The Bible says there is a time and place for all things, and that in all things we must use wisdom. Meaning, There will be a time and a place to use scripture or use a word to encourage or enlighten someone who may be going through something, but constantly beating people about the head is not what GOD intended for us to do. Because remember, if you have a hand in leading someone astray from Him, you will be charged for that. Every single thing out of your mouth and or your Facebook Page doesn't have to be God this and God that. We get it, It's like what are you trying to prove and to who? We just ask that you come down every once in a while so us mere mortals can have a regular conversation with you about regular stuff.

Don't waste your time and energy trying to prove your value or worth on someone who can't or refuse to see all the good that you represent and bring to your relationship. True love is not measurable by anything we can see, nor should it ever come with a price tag. Time lost can never be regained, so don't waste it. If you've been with someone for a while and still have to ask "where are you" in the relationship? That's a huge red flag right there. You have to learn the difference between being patient and letting things develop naturally, over time, or when you're simply being strung along. If they don't appreciate your presence, your absence would bring clarity and closure, in the spirit of goodbye.

IN RELATIONSHIPS, KNOW YOUR ROLES AND PLAY YOUR POSITIONS
CHAPTER 35

When a man and woman come together in a union, If its ordained by God, marriage is not far off because that's what He ordains, and why the union is referred to as "Holy Matrimony", because in God's eyesight, marriage is holy and regarded as sacred to Him. Let me go back just a little to give some subtext to this segment. When God created man, he gave him dominion and full rulership of the earth, but when he saw that man was alone, this was not good, and felt man should not be alone and he therefore created Adam a help mate and called her name Eve; she was woman because she came from the womb of man or Adam's rib. When Eve was tricked and convinced by the serpent to eat of the tree of life for which God said they should not eat, she then tempted and convinced Adam to eat, he did, now they both had officially transgressed and disobeyed God. Now, when God discovered this, because Eve had essentially tempted Adam to eat and caused him to transgress, God said in Genesis 3:23 "Unto the woman He said, I will greatly multiply thy sorrow and thy conception; in sorrow thou shalt bring forth children; and thy desire shall be to thy husband, and he shall rule over thee"...Ok, this is where and why women have excruciating labor pains til this day. That last line, when He said "thy desire shall be to thy husband, and he shall rule over thee" "rule" was the word translated from Hebrew, But essentially God was making Adam the "head" or leader of the woman and his family. This is His ordained order, and in this there is no debate or doubt unless you are simply a non-believer. Now, let me break this down. The Universal Order of things dictates that there is a masculine and a feminine, ok cool. God making Adam the head or leader of the woman does not make her subservient or change the initial role she was created for in the first place, which was to do what? Be a helpmate. That said, the roles for men and women were established and ordained by God. What I want you all to understand is, that submission does not mean subservient. For some reason, and no pastor or bishop ever teaches this or touches on it, but just call me Mr. "Keep it real" because that's exactly what I am always going to do. But in Ephesians 5:21 it clearly states, "Submitting yourselves one to another in the fear of God", which essentially means husbands and wives should submit to each other. The problem is this, when the average woman hears the word submit or submission, she automatically, and incorrectly assumes that it means she should be subservient and "lesser" than the man, and men, if they're told they should submit to their wives as well ,the first thing they would most likely think is that they're not a "punk" to be submitting to a woman; and that is incorrect and the wrong attitude as well. Consider this, to help illustrate my point; Abraham submitted to Sarah; When Sarah wanted Hagar and Ishmael to leave because she didn't like how he was treating Isaac, it grieved Abraham because Ishmael was still his son, he loved him and didn't want to send him away like that; but Sarah was his wife, and remember I said how God ordains and honors marriage, and how it's sacred to Him? Well, He told Abraham to listen to his wife and send Ishmael and his mother away, and that He would take care of Ishmael and make him the leader of a great nation. As you all may or may not know, that great nation was the Arabs, originally called The Ishmaelites, they are extremely wealthy and as a people have never been conquered. In that situation, Abraham submitted to his wife, and sent Ishmael and his mother away as she requested. Abraham doing that, lines up perfectly with what Ephesians 5:21, with respect to husbands and wives submitting to each other.

See, it's not about either party playing any kind of subservient role or nothing like that. Submitting i.e. respecting, walking side by side as one flesh, is acceptable and actually encouraged by God. We all have a role to play, culturally even, as men and as women we have placed each other in certain roles, and there is absolutely nothing wrong with this. When it's time to cut the grass, change the oil or the tire, take out the trash, etc...ladies, let's be honest, the majority of you are not going to do those things, why? Because as a society and as a culture we have regulated those roles to men, and again, there is nothing wrong with that. Know your roles and play your position. There is a masculine and a feminine. If there is an intruder in the house, and a woman and her husband is lying in the bed, ladies, are you going to get up and confront the intruder or expect your husband to? Right, because one of his roles as head of that house and as the leader of his family is to protect, bottom line. So let's get away from this fallacy and mentality that there is no gender roles in a home, that is an unhealthy mindset. Ladies, your job as queen is to help your king lead. You treat and respect him like the king he was designed to be, as long as he is relishing in that role and not simply because he has a penis. No, you do not treat a man like a king who insists on acting like a joker. His action (s) dictates that. There are two roles in a household, the husband and the wife, both can't play the husband role, that role is reserved for the man. Fall back ladies, let him be that, you be the queen that you were meant to be, and now your household is in order, and ready to receive the abundant blessings of God. When all hell breaks loose in your home, and nothing seems to be going right, look no further than your house being out of order as the culprit. At the end of the day, we all simply have to know our roles, and play our positions. There's no harm in that and don't let anyone tell you any differently. Ideally, everyone has a role to play, even our children; no-one is exempt. Having and maintaining a balanced family takes a collective effort.

REFERENCES

Universal Laws, (2012) Retrieved from
http://www.abundance-and-happiness.com/universal-laws.htmlUniversal Laws, (N.D.) Retrieved from
http://www.totalpresence.org/universal-laws.phpDecans in
Astrology- Planetary Rulers, Retrieved from
http://www.horoscopeswithin.com/decans.php
Capricorn Star Sign, (2015) Retrieved from
http://www.alizons-psychic-secrets.com/capricorn.html
Centaurs, (2009) Retrieved from
http://monsters.monstrous.com/centaurs.htm
Capricorn Man and Capricorn Woman Compatibility, (2015)
Retrieved from
http://www.ask-oracle.com/sign-compatibility/capricorn-man-capricorn-woman/

ABOUT THE AUTHOR

Dr. Manifest originally hails from Charleston, South Carolina. He spent some formative years in San Diego, California and currently resides in Fayetteville, North Carolina. He is a U.S. Navy Veteran, single, educated, and holds several Undergraduate Degrees (in Business and Criminal Justice, currently on path to his PhD in Psychology). He studied astrology in a self-taught capacity, with an emphasis In Capricorn for over 8 years and is considered a "specialist" in this field. With years of interviews, research and recorded data under his belt, all of the aforementioned has been extremely instrumental in his development within the astrology "discipline". He has always had a wide range of interests ever since he was a child and the many different things he writes about is indicative of that, plus lines up with his 'Capricornian' nature of not wanting to ever be placed inside a box. Within the astrology discipline, he studied everything from astrological chart interpretation to compatibility assessments. His expertise is highly sought out, appreciated and respected. He is an esteemed member of Sigma Beta Delta (an International Honor Society) he's multi-talented, extremely gifted and has always had a "way with words" even as a song writer and music producer; He's built up quite a loyal and respectable fan base for his many writings and "Words of Wisdom"... Dealing with everything from human behavior (using astrology as a behavioral science), relationships, inspirational, self-help and different aspects of philosophy, theology, black history (using DNA and genetics) to domestic violence intervention, for which he has a certificate in as well. The inspiration for this book came about when he created a community for Capricorns on Facebook and called it The Capricorn Connection. His and the community's popularity sky-rocketed due to his uncanny accuracy, knowledge and insight into the minds and ways of Capricorn. He built that community from the ground up and gradually his credibility was proven and established as legitimate. There is no other community or website like it in existence, and this book will certainly cement his position and this proclamation.

Made in the USA
Middletown, DE
09 May 2020